QUICK SMART START

SIXTEEN USEFUL TRUTHS FOR NEW FOLLOWERS OF CHRIST

DOUG BURRIER

Copyright © 2018,2020,2022 by Doug Burrier

All rights reserved. No portion of this publication may be reproduced, distributed, or transmitted in any form or by any means, or stored in a database or retrieval system, without the prior written permission from the publisher, except as permitted by U.S. copyright law. For permissions, contact: permissions@different.ly.

Published 2022 by Different.ly Publishing

4443 Westside Farm Place
Acworth, Ga. 30101
www.different.ly

ISBN: 978-1-7334021-4-9

Second Edition.

Printed in the United States of America

Sustainable Discipleship® is a registered Service Mark of Doug Burrier

Unless otherwise indicated, all Scripture quotations are taken from the HOLY BIBLE, NEW LIVING TRANSLATION Copyright © 1996 by Tyndale Charitable Trust. All rights reserved.

Scripture quotations marked (NASU) are from THE NEW AMERICAN STANDARD BIBLE UPDATE. Copyright © 1960, 1962, 1963, 1968, 1971, 1972, 1973, 1975, 1977, 1995, by The Lockman Foundation. Used by permission. All rights reserved.
Scripture quotations marked (KJV) are from The King James Version
Copyright © 1988-2003, by Biblesoft, Inc. All rights reserved.
Scripture quotations marked (NCV) are from NEW CENTURY VERSION
Copyright © 1987, 1988, 1991 by Word Publishing,
a division of Thomas Nelson, Inc. All rights reserved.
Scripture quotations marked (HCSB) are from the HOLMAN CHRISTIAN STANDARD BIBLE®
Copyright © 1999, 2000, 2002, 2003 by Holman Bible Publishers All rights reserved.
Scripture quotations marked (NIV) are from the HOLY BIBLE, NEW INTERNATIONAL VERSION ®
Copyright © 1973, 1978, 1984 by International Bible Society. Used by permission of Zondervan Publishing House. All rights reserved.
Scripture quotations marked (TEV) are from the Today's English Version First Edition
Copyright © 1976. American Bible Society. Used by permission.

We gratefully credit RIBBI International that, years ago, shared their source text for a discipleship booklet guide. Their work spurned an outline and research that grew into this guide. They were one of many invaluable resources and great disciple making partners. A donation is made to RIBBI efforts for every purchase of this guide.

Table of Contents

Introduction		1
TRUTH 1	Your Relationship with God	5
TRUTH 2	Eternal Security	21
TRUTH 3	Baptism	33
TRUTH 4	The Bible	43
TRUTH 5	The Holy Spirit	59
TRUTH 6	Prayer	73
TRUTH 7	The Will of God	87
TRUTH 8	The Church	101
TRUTH 9	Other Christians	119
TRUTH 10	Living Among the World	135
TRUTH 11	The Workplace	151
TRUTH 12	Tithes and Offerings	165
TRUTH 13	Material Possessions	181
TRUTH 14	Sin	193
TRUTH 15	Freedom from Judgement	211
TRUTH 16	Jesus Comes Back	225
About Us		243
Acknowledgments		245
About the Author		247
More Resources		247

Anyone who listens to my teaching and follows it is wise, like a person who builds a house on solid rock. Though the rain comes in torrents and the floodwaters rise and the winds beat against that house, it won't collapse because it is built on bedrock. But anyone who hears my teaching and doesn't obey it is foolish, like a person who builds a house on sand. When the rains and floods come and the winds beat against that house, it will collapse with a mighty crash.

Jesus
Matthew 7:24-27

Introduction

I have no idea how you are feeling as you pick up this book and start reading it, but I am almost certain you are curious. Curious about what to do with your new faith. Curious about whether you started your walk with Jesus well. Or curious why, after all these years, your small group leader handed you a book about starting.

I remember my start. It was anything but quick and smart. Like many of you, I got busy at church after my salvation. I went to Bible Studies and Sunday School, helped with Vacation Bible School, chaperoned camps, and served on Sundays. But I struggled with so many things.

I struggled with old habits and temptations. I remember wondering if I was really saved when I read, "No one who believes in me will continue to sin." Could I lose my salvation? Had I lost it? I also remember not wanting to tell anyone that I was struggling. They seemed to have it all together, and I didn't.

I heard people say, "God told me to ..." wondering why I did not hear God that clearly. Why could I not hear him? Was I praying correctly? Was God not talking to me because I did something wrong? Again, I remember not wanting to say anything.

I read about God creating the world and wrestled with what I had been taught about evolution. I wondered if some of my answered prayers weren't just coincidences.

One guy told me that I needed to be filled with the Holy Spirit and speak in tongues (see 1 Corinthians 14:2). He invited me to a prayer service where everyone prayed for me to receive the Holy Spirit and speak in a new angelic language. After hours of seeking, praying, and listening, I finally uttered a few gibberish words. They were so excited. I felt nothing. I was a fake. I wondered, "Is this why I got saved? Is something wrong with me?"

My new teachers wanted me to get rid of my few worldly friends. They worried that I would succumb to temptation and return to my old ways. Little did they know that I was falling into temptation and doing "wrong" stuff with my new church friends. We did the right stuff and then went and did the wrong stuff. Had I really changed? Was God mad at me?

Life kept happening, and decisions had to be made. Should I follow my heart and look for a new job? Could I date a girl who wasn't churchy? And, then later, how should I raise my daughter? Should I make her go to church?

Church people told me all the answers were in the Bible. But I couldn't find clear answers. I really wanted to do this right. I wanted God to be happy with me. I was struggling, and I almost became one of those people who got saved, couldn't live it, quit, and faded off into the world.

Have you ever felt this way? Do you feel this way? If you are a new believer in Jesus, I would love to tell you that you won't struggle. But I can't. Anyone who decides to begin following God will struggle. Everything new is a struggle. We get sore when we start to exercise and get in shape. We struggle as we lose weight. We struggle as we learn new things. We struggle as we grow in relationships. It is okay to struggle as we start.

But that kind of struggle wasn't what I was dealing with.

I was struggling with a lack of information. I was struggling with a lack of confidence. I was struggling to figure out where to start. Most of the "Christian" answers were for me to go do something, get involved, and study the Bible. I was doing all those things, but I still had a thousand more questions.

Looking back, it is easy to see that I needed some quick, smart, useful answers to move me forward. In fact, that is exactly how I started figuring this whole Christian thing out. I found answers to my questions one by one and moved on to the next. But it was a slow go (way too slow) with way too many failures. I have so many regrets from those years. But here's the good news, getting answers doesn't have to be that slow. Starting doesn't have to be an unhealthy struggle. You don't have to have a lack of information.

The Bible does have most of the answers to your questions. And when God's words don't address your questions directly (like who to date), the concepts and principles in God's words will help you answer them. But it takes time to read the Bible. It takes time to absorb and connect all that truth. So how do you get a quicker, smarter start? You cheat.

And that is what this book is - it is a cheat sheet for people starting, restarting, and refreshing their walk with Jesus. It is a cheat sheet for those who want to help others get started. I wrote this book - to help you cheat. To help bring some quick Biblical answers to questions you have, should have, or will ask soon. The answers are simple. There is no opinion or conjecture. It is just a shortcut to help you get quick, smart Biblical answers about your relationship with God.

More than anything, I want you to get the quick, smart start that I needed. I want you to be prepared, confident, and skilled in navigating struggles as they come. I want to share some principles of Christianity that will propel you forward and accelerate your experience with God. I want to answer a few of those standard questions we all seem to have when we start following God. Without a doubt, these aren't all the answers! But after years of listening to others as they start, these are the top sixteen topics that come up again and again.

These answers have helped hundreds of people already. I promise you that these sixteen truths will jump-start your faith into action. And that is important because I bet you really want to get this right.

How to Use this Book

There is actually a bit of science in how this workbook is put together. It is designed to work the way your brain works. Let me explain that design without getting too caught up in the science of learning. When it comes to new concepts, we learn and remember best when we process the information in smaller quantities over a period of time. Why? When we learn, our brains build pathways of information. Each path ends with the big truth (or concept), and supporting facts get stored along the way. You strengthen a learning pathway by studying the same end truth over and over, adding new facts to the pathway each time. Simply put, the more traveled the pathway, the easier it is to remember.

With this in mind, the best way to use this workbook is to work through **one lesson a week**. Each day, **do one section of that week's lesson** and **practice that week's memory verse**. Once you complete all the sections for a week, use the remaining days to review what you have learned and to practice your memory verse.

You may not like memorizing (I didn't), but I cannot emphasize the power of memorizing enough. The verses you memorize will become the anchor (or big concept) at the end of each week's learning pathway. They will become a road sign in your brain that helps you remember the concept and all the truths you learn along the way. So practice your memory verses along the way.

If you are having trouble memorizing, try this trick. Read the verse, write it, read what you wrote out loud, then try to say the verse without looking at it. Make sure you get the week's verse correct at least once daily. At least once a week, recite all the verses you have memorized.

The truths in this workbook are found in the Bible. Some verses are included in the text. Some verse references are provided in parenthesis like this (see verse). **Looking up the verse references is important** because God's truths are what you need. It will also help you figure out where to find things in your Bible. Some verse references appear in bold, blue like this (see **verse**). Those verses are provided in the margin for quick reference.

This workbook works excellently for individuals but even better in groups. Why? When a group gathers together to share what God showed them, God uses the variety of learning styles and insights to give each group member a broader understanding of that week's truth. It is like your learning goes exponential. Men and women have different perspectives. Older and wiser are inspired by younger and fresh eyes. The truth God spoke to one person adds to the truth that he spoke to another. There is power in the variety of Christians. Who should lead the discussion? Anyone. The goal is to review, not teach. The leader only needs to guide the group to listen to what God has taught each person. So get a few friends, and get a quicker, smarter start following God.

If you need any help, the folks at Sustainable Discipleship are ready. Just reach out at team@sustainable-discipleship.com.

TRUTH 1

MEMORY VERSE

Jesus answered, "I tell you the truth, unless you are born again, you cannot be in God's kingdom. Humans can only reproduce human life, but the Spirit gives birth to spiritual life."

John 3:3

Your Relationship with God

One Step at a Time

I remember my first year of being married to Amber. She was so intelligent, independent, and successful. I loved those things about her until we moved in together.

I had ways of doing things that made sense to me. For example, I am a systematic cleaner, always thinking ahead. I do whatever needs to be done along the way to the next room, never wasting a step. Amber was what I would call a chaotic cleaner. She would get distracted and finish everything a little bit at a time. It didn't make sense. She is one of those people who eats one part of their meal at a time. Why was she so systematic eating and so chaotic cleaning?

She was also super systematic about loading the dishwasher. Whereas I was a chaotic dish loader. It drove her crazy until I changed my ways.

There were so many things that we did not know about each other until we started living together. It is the same for every new relationship. We enter those relationships motivated by love or friendship. We see the value. We like the person. But the more intimate a relationship and the more you are together - the more challenges come. It takes time to make compromises, understand the person, and learn from the good in them.

When you ask God to save you, he does just that. He rescues you by forgiving your sins. He puts his Spirit in your heart and makes you a new person. It's pretty wild if you think about it. God's Spirit is in me? Yes. He doesn't see me as a sinner? No. He made me a new creature? Yes. He sees me as part of his family? Yes.

When you get saved, God brings you into a relationship with him. And it is not just a friendship — you are family. He calls himself your Father. Jesus calls you his brother. And this new relationship changes everything.

You have a new lease on life. You have a new power in your heart. God actually says that the old you was put to death when you became a Christian. He calls it being "born again." It is a word picture of you entering his family as a new child.

But if you are like me, your new relationship is bringing a lot of adjustment and a lot of questions. Will he leave me? What if I don't get things right the first time? What is this new relationship all about?

It is crucial that you understand your new relationship with God. It is vital that you know what a steady, patient Father he is. And that's our focus for this week.

QUICK, SMART START

TWO SPIRITUAL FAMILIES

John 3:3,6

Jesus answered, "I tell you the truth, unless you are born again, you cannot be in God's kingdom. Humans can only reproduce human life, but the Spirit gives birth to spiritual life."

Everything about your spiritual life is, well, spiritual. You have probably heard the Christian phrase "born again," but you may not know why it is used. Jesus once said, "Unless you are born again, you can not enter the Kingdom of God." An intelligent Jewish leader replied, "How can an old man go back into his mother's womb?"

Jesus explained, "Humans can only reproduce human life, but the Spirit gives birth to spiritual life." The new relationship that you have with God is spiritual. The new family you are a part of is spiritual. It is a spiritual relationship. John explained this about you and me when we became Christians.

> But to all who believed him and accepted him, he gave the right to become children of God. They are reborn—not with a physical birth resulting from human passion or plan, but a birth that comes from God.
>
> John 1:12-13

And that kind of makes sense - right? But did you know that before you became part of God's spiritual family, you were part of another spiritual family? It might sound a bit scary, but two spiritual families are going on all around us. A group of people was claiming to be children of Abraham, children of God when Jesus said this to them,

> If God were your Father, you would love me, because I have come to you from God. I am not here on my own, but he sent me. Why can't you understand what I am saying? It's because you can't even hear me! For you are the children of your father the devil, you love to do the evil things he does."
>
> John 8:42-44

According to Jesus, every person is in one of two families and has one of two fathers: God or the devil.

The Devil's Family

Everyone enters this family by physical birth. It is the original "spiritual" family tree with Adam at the top. Adam was the first man. Eve was the first woman. God created them. Life was perfect until they both chose to sin. and then, everything changed. Their lives were drastically different, and, according to the Bible, they died spiritually. They lost their spiritual oneness with God, and they became corrupted. Their original design was forever broken, and we inherited their imperfection.

Everyone is born with a sinful nature. No one has to teach us to do wrong. On the contrary, parents, teachers, and leaders invest in teaching us how to live well because we are prone to err. We are prone to selfishness. We are prone to be distant from God. It is natural for us to do our own thing. You inherited your sinful nature from your distant ancestor, Adam, because he decided to disobey God. It is a physical and spiritual consequence of the first sin. Paul, an incredible Christian teacher, puts it this way in the Bible,

> Therefore, just as sin entered the world through one man, and death through sin, in this way death spread to all men, because all sinned.
> Romas 5:12 HCSB

Paul teaches us that, as a result of sin, we were sentenced to die.

> ...so death passed on to all men.
> Romans 5:12 NASB

> The wages of sin is death....
> Romans 6:23 NASB

> ...In Adam all die....
> 1 Corinthians 15:22 NASB

But, your choice to believe in God and follow him changed everything. Becoming a Christian began your return to God's original design, which changed your very nature. You became part of a new inheritance and part of a new family tree.

God's Family

Everyone who believes in God enters this family. You became part of God's family by spiritual birth when you became a follower of Christ. We have already seen how Jesus explained it to a prominent Jewish leader in your memory verse for this week.

❶ Write out your memory verse for this week.

_____

_____

_____

_____

Spiritual birth puts you into God's family in the same way your physical birth puts you into your earthly family.

Spiritual birth puts you into God's family in the same way your physical birth puts you into your earthly family. You are now a child of God by birth and have inherited God's divine nature. You have eternal life.

> I tell you the truth, whoever believes has eternal life.
>
> John 6:47 NCV

> The one who believes in the Son has eternal life ....
>
> John 3:36 HCSB

> The one who has the Son has life....
>
> 1 John 5:12 HCSB

Being in God's family separates you from the devil's family. God's Spirit now lives inside you (1 Corinthians 6:19). You get to live a new life, different from those who do not follow God (2 Corinthians 6:14-18). Paul summarized your new relationship this way,

> If anyone belongs to Christ, there is a new creation. The old things have gone; everything is made new! All this is from God. Through Christ, God made peace between us and himself....
>
> 2 Corinthians 5:17-18 NASB

You inherited your worldly nature from Adam. Paul describes this at the "outer man" or "flesh." Your body is the same after salvation, but your spirit is born again, made alive, and joined with God's spirit. You are a new person, a new creation.

Again, Paul explains this new birth and relationship,

> Therefore, put to death what belongs to your worldly nature: sexual immorality, impurity, lust, evil desire, and greed, which is idolatry. Because of these, God's wrath comes on the disobedient, and you once walked in these things when you were living in them. But now you must also put away all the following: anger, wrath, malice, slander, and filthy language from your mouth. Do not lie to one another, since you have put off the old self with its practices and have put on the new self. You are being renewed in knowledge according to the image of your Creator.
> Colossians 3:5-10 HCSB

You will be free from your flesh when you stand in God's presence (after your body dies). But until then, you have a task ahead of you - adjusting your life and your body to follow God's truths. The Spirit of God lives in you now. And he will continue to help you change. He will continue to teach you what is right and convict you of what is wrong. He will continue to empower you.

> Therefore we do not give up; even though our outer person is being destroyed, our inner person is being renewed day by day. For our momentary light affliction is producing for us an absolutely incomparable eternal weight of glory. So we do not focus on what is seen, but on what is unseen; for what is seen is temporary, but what is unseen is eternal.
> 2 Corinthians 4:16-18 HCSB

The Holy Spirit and God's truths about great living are the fuel to move from the old life to the new.

❷ How does someone become part of the devil's family?

_____

_____

❸ How does someone become part of God's family?

_____

_____

_____

Romans 3:23

all have sinned and fall short of the glory of God

④ Why are people sentenced to die after their physical (first) birth?

_____

_____

⑤ What type of life is promised to those in God's family?

_____

_____

Romans 6:23

For the wages of sin is death, but the gracious gift of God is eternal life in Christ Jesus our Lord.

The two spiritual fathers are the devil and God. We are born into the devil's family because of Adam's sin (see **Romans 3:23, 6:23**). But when we believe in God, we are reborn spiritually and receive eternal life. You are part of a new family and in a new relationship with God.

WHAT IS MY RELATIONSHIP WITH GOD NOW?

Since the beginning, God has presented himself to humans in three ways:

- As Father
- As Jesus, the Son of God
- As the Holy Spirit

From our perspective of time and space, each presentation of God has a specific purpose. In an oversimplified way, we can say the Father sent the Son, the Son brought salvation, and the Spirit is our daily guide. All three, the Father, the Son, and the Spirit, are God. Old school Christians referred to God this way: God the Father, God the Son, and God the Holy Spirit.

So your relationship with God has three very real dimensions. God is your Heavenly Father, and you are His child. Jesus is your Savior, and you are Jesus' sibling. The Holy Spirit is your guide and lives within you.

Your relationship with God is like the earthly relationship between a good father and his child. As Father, God no longer interacts with you as a sinner or someone foreign to him. He interacts with you as his child.

- A good father cares for his children. 1 Peter 5:7
- A good father protects his children. Matthew 18:6
- A good father provides for his children. Philippians 4:19
- A good father guides and teaches his children. John 14:26
- A good father helps his children. Psalm 46:1
- A good father strengthens his children. Philippians 4:13
- A good father disciplines his children. Hebrews 12:5-11
- A good father feeds his children. Matthew 6:31-33
- A good father has a plan for his children. Romans 8:28-29

God is your Father. Jesus is your advocate. The Holy Spirit is your realtime guide on earth.

A good father never does anything to hurt his child. God only does those things that will help His children grow and mature. Unlike earthly fathers, God never makes a mistake in His dealings with His children.

> If you then, being evil, know how to give good gifts unto your children, how much more shall your Father which is in heaven give good things to them that ask him?
>
> Matthew 7:11 NASB

Jesus walked the earth, but now he is in heaven, and one of his principal roles is to be your advocate. The one which presents your salvation before the Father. John, one of the original followers of God, writes,

> My little children, I am writing these things to you so that you may not sin. And if anyone sins, we have an Advocate with the Father, Jesus Christ the righteous.
>
> 1 John 2:1 NASB

After reading this week's verses, it is easy to see God as Father and Savior to you. We know what fathers and saviors are. It can be more challenging to see God as Spirit. There is nothing in this physical world that puts the Spirit into context. Your relationship with God's Spirit is intimate. The Spirit lives inside you. Before salvation, he convicted you that you were wrong. He convicted you that God was real and that Jesus rose from the dead to forgive your sins. Now God's Spirit lives within you in an inexplicable, miraculous way. We will talk more about the Spirit in Lesson 5. For now, know that the Spirit is your guide in truth and your connection to God.

> But the Helper will teach you everything and will cause you to remember all that I told you. This Helper is the Holy Spirit whom the Father will send in my name.
>
> John 14:26

When God speaks, he speaks His words through His Spirit into your innermost being.

> I have many more things to say to you, but they are too much for you now. But when the Spirit of truth comes, he will lead you into all truth. He will not speak his own words, but he will speak only what he hears, and he will tell you what is to come. The Spirit of truth will bring glory to me, because he will take what I have to say and tell it to you. All that the Father has is mine. That is why I said that the Spirit will take what I have to say and tell it to you.
>
> John 16:12-15

6 Your new relationship with God can be seen through the earthly father and child relationship. List five ways God deals with you as His child.

_____

_____

_____

_____

_____

WHAT IS MY PART IN THIS RELATIONSHIP?

Day 3

Your part in this relationship is to be a follower, a child. You do not have to know everything at every moment. In fact, it is almost certain that you will not know everything exactly when you think you need to know it.

> Your relationship toward God is one of total surrender and following.

In other words, relax. Do not overthink it. Just do what you did the moment you believed in God - surrender to the Truth. Commit yourself to follow God's instructions for life. Commit yourself to know all the great things about who God is, what he likes, and what he does. And commit yourself to become more and more like him. Be devoted.

The greatest mistake people make when it comes to their relationship with God is forgetting the beginning. Do you remember that moment when you realized that God was God? Do you remember how overwhelming it was to realize that He was all-knowing, all-loving, and all-powerful? Do you remember how you were willing to do anything to be a part of his family?

That is surrender, total surrender. It is the beginning, the journey, and the end of our relationship with God. He is God, and he longs to bless us. He wants to guide you so much that he put his wisdom in print. Yes, the Bible tells us how to live. So as you learn, stay surrendered, apply the truths you learn, and obey. Be his child. Be his servant. Be a follower.

7 How is your relationship with God different now than before you were part of God's family?

_____

_____

_____

_____

QUICK, SMART START

WILL I SIN?

It is natural to struggle as you exchange old habits and lifestyles for a better way. But, you do not have to sin.

Will you sin? Yes and no. It is almost certain that you will sin after salvation -- intentionally or unintentionally. But, in reality, you do not have to sin. God's instructions to us are for our benefit. He is the Creator and Lord. He knows what is good for us and bad and why we struggle to do what is good. He knows and loves us, and he never desired us to struggle with sin.

When you start following God, there is so much that you do not know about God's character, his desires for you, what is good for you, and what is bad. This is one of the greatest startup challenges. You learn something new and realize, "Holy cow! I am doing that. I didn't even know it was wrong." There are other times when you will know something is wrong and struggle to not do it. Aligning ourselves with God and adjusting our old ways, our old brain, and our old habits can take a little time. It is a process. Even the great followers of God have struggled as their old ways and flesh adjusted to the new life and nature God gave him. Paul, a passionate follower, said,

> I can will it, but I can't do it. I decide to do good, but I don't really do it; I decide not to do bad, but then I do it anyway. My decisions, such as they are, don't result in actions. Something has gone wrong deep within me and gets the better of me every time. It happens so regularly that it's predictable. The moment I decide to do good, sin is there to trip me up. I truly delight in God's commands, but it's pretty obvious that not all of me joins in that delight. Parts of me covertly rebel, and just when I least expect it, they take charge. I've tried everything and nothing helps. I'm at the end of my rope. Is there no one who can do anything for me? Isn't that the real question? The answer, thank God, is that Jesus Christ can and does. He acted to set things right in this life of contradictions where I want to serve God with all my heart and mind, but am pulled by the influence of sin to do something totally different.
>
> Romans 7:17-25 MSG

You do not know what you do not know. You are beginning to learn God's truths for exceptional living. Like a child learning to walk, you will learn some lessons along the way. You will try to live well and struggle. You will do things that God does not want for you. You may even intentionally do something wrong. The struggle is natural as you exchange old habits and lifestyles for a better way. But, you do not have to sin.

You have always had the power to choose. Before you became a Christian, you chose whatever you wanted — good or bad. You did not have the Spirit of God in you to help you know what is best. You did not have the miraculous power of God to support and strengthen you. But, now you have the Spirit, and he can convict you (convince you) or warn you (that feeling deep inside) that something is wrong before you sin. The Spirit, God, will talk to you, and you can follow your heart even when you may not have learned the truth. We do not have to sin when we embrace surrender, when we listen to the Spirit, and when we follow.

HOW DOES SIN AFFECT MY NEW RELATIONSHIP?

Day 5

An easy way to understand the effect of sin on your relationship with God is to look at the relationship between a loving parent and a child. Loving parents give good instruction and direction to their children. The good parent wants the child to have a good life today and the best possible future as an adult. The good parent wants the child to be safe and avoid needless pain. So, a good parent teaches truths that lead to success, prosperity, safety, wisdom, and peace.

Good parents discipline their children. They want their child to understand what he did wrong, why it was wrong, and admit it was wrong. Good parents do not disown or disgrace disobedient children. Good parents know that we are not the wrongs we do. But good parents do want the child to know the action was wrong. Why? Because when a child admits his actions were wrong, good parents can now guide him. Good parents want their children to see the value of doing good. They want their children to choose things that lead to a great life. They want the best for their child.

1 John 1:6-10

So we are lying if we say we have fellowship with God but go on living in spiritual darkness; we are not practicing the truth. But if we are living in the light, as God is in the light, then we have fellowship with each other, and the blood of Jesus, his Son, cleanses us from all sin. If we claim we have no sin, we are only fooling ourselves and not living in the truth. But if we confess our sins to him, he is faithful and just to forgive us our sins and to cleanse us from all wickedness.

God is the ultimate good parent. You will always be his child. He will always love you. He will always hope for you. He will convict you, tell you when you do wrong. He will teach you the best ways to succeed and thrive on earth. He longs for you to understand the value of following his ways. In fact, he has an entire book that illustrates and shows you the best way to live - the Bible.

God is always your good Father. God is always your advocate (Jesus). He will always guide you with his Spirit. If you sin, your relationship does not change. But, he will discipline you as his child.

> "My child, don't make light of the Lord's discipline, and don't give up when he corrects you. For the Lord disciplines those he loves, and he punishes each one he accepts as his child." As you endure this divine discipline, remember that God is treating you as his own children. Who ever heard of a child who is never disciplined by its father? If God doesn't discipline you as he does all of his children, it means that you are illegitimate and are not really his children at all. Since we respected our earthly fathers who disciplined us, shouldn't we submit even more to the discipline of the Father of our spirits, and really live? For our earthly fathers disciplined us for a few years, doing the best they knew how. But God's discipline is always good for us, so that we might share in his holiness. No discipline is enjoyable while it is happening—it's painful! But afterward there will be a peaceful harvest of right living for those who are trained in this way.
>
> Hebrews 12:5-11 NLT

If you sin, God will continue investing in you as much as you allow him. He will teach you. And, He is always ready to forgive, reconcile, and get you back on the right path.

❽ When a Christian chooses to continue in a particular sin, what can he expect from God?

_____

_____

YOUR RELATIONSHIP WITH GOD

WHAT SHOULD I DO WHEN I SIN?

When you sin, you should make it right. You should own your error and apologize. This is how you keep your relationship healthy. God teaches us to confess our sins and trust the blood of Jesus Christ to cleanse us (see 1 John 1:6-10). That means we believe that when Jesus gave his life to forgive our sins, he actually forgave them. Holding and hiding your sins will never lead to a full life (see Proverbs 28:13). Talk with God honestly and ask for help.

Proverbs 28:13

People who conceal their sins will not prosper, but if they confess and turn from them, they will receive mercy.

9 According to God's words in 1 John 1:9, when we confess our sins to God, what two things does God do?

_____

_____

HOW CAN I AVOID SIN?

The easiest way to avoid sin is to focus all your time on doing the good things God desires. It is a simple equation, I cannot follow God and not follow simultaneously. Another way to avoid sinning is to dump the old life you lived before becoming a Christian. It helps to stay away from the wrong places and the wrong people as you start your new life (see Ephesians 4:22).

But even when we follow and guard ourselves, sin can still easily surprise us. It can be beneficial to know what sin is. And the simplest way to identify sin is to know the three ways to sin.

Ephesians 4:22

You were taught to leave your old self—to stop living the evil way you lived before. That old self becomes worse, because people are fooled by the evil things they want to do.

17

The Three Ways to Sin

- **Doing something that God says you should not do**— something that is not good for you or those around you.
- **Not doing something that God says you should do** — something that is good for you or those around you (see **James 4:17**).
- **Doing things that you are not sure of** — not acting in faith (see **Romans 14:23**).

Learning God's ideal ways for your life is the best way to avoid sin. You are powerful when you know what is good for you and what is not. It is pretty easy to figure out the things **you should not do** (murder, gossip, cheat, etc.). As you start reading the Bible, you will quickly see the things God says **you should do** (be generous, forgive, help others, etc.). But what about the things you are not sure of?

The last way to sin (**doing a doubt**) can seem confusing, but understanding what sin is clears it up. Sin is not following God. If God says, "Don't," and you do, you are not following. It is a sin. If God says, "Do," and you do not do, you are not following God. It is a sin.

In the same way, if you are not sure (if you are guessing), you are not really following God. So what do you do when you are not sure? Ask someone smart for a Bible verse or truth. Or, simply wait. No matter your decision, you want to be sure that you follow God and apply his truths.

10 Take a minute and write this week's memory verse.

_____

_____

_____

_____

_____

James 4:17

So for one who knows the right thing to do and does not do it, for him it is sin.

Romans 14:23

Anything that is done without believing it is right is a sin. (NCV)

For whatever does not proceed from faith is sin. (ESV)

YOUR RELATIONSHIP WITH GOD

AT THE END OF THE WEEK ANSWER THESE QUESTIONS

What was the most meaningful statement(s) or scripture this week?

_____
_____
_____
_____
_____
_____

Reword the statement or scripture into a prayer of response to God.

_____
_____
_____
_____
_____
_____

What actions do you need to take in response to this week's study?

_____
_____
_____
_____
_____
_____

TRUTH 2

MEMORY VERSE

And this is the will of God, that I should not lose even one of all those he has given me, but that I should raise them up at the last day.

John 6:37

Eternal Security

Am I Really Saved?

"I, uh, don't know if I am saved," Karla said, trembling. I winced inside. I knew this feeling from long ago. I knew this question, this struggle. I have heard this question hundreds of times. And, to be honest, I have sometimes wondered if the people asking were saved.

When our outside lives do not align with what we say we believe, "Am I really saved?" becomes a very real question. I remember the first years of my Christianity. I struggled with so many things. I had habits that the church said were wrong that I could not seem to stop. I fell back into old dating patterns and anger and did things I knew were wrong. At times, I was convicted but did not change. I believed in God, but clearly, I was not adjusting my life to his truths. I felt so guilty.

It got worse when I read, "He who loves me will not continue to sin," and worried. Did I really love Jesus? Was I saved? I remembered the incredible moment of surrender when I asked him to save me. I could remember the forgiveness. No, there was no doubt. I meant it, I felt it, I got saved. But my continued struggles made me wonder if I had somehow lost my salvation. I was not alone; if you have this question, you are not alone. Almost every new believer faces this doubt. The short answer is "No. You cannot lose your salvation." That is our focus this week.

QUICK, SMART START

HOW CAN I KNOW FOR SURE THAT I AM SAVED?

Almost every Christian has wondered whether they were "really saved" at some point. The journey from living independently to following God is a big adjustment. It is natural to wonder if you are saved as you struggle to make better choices. John, a passionate follower of Jesus, wrote an entire letter about this question. He tells Christians,

> I have written these things to you who believe in the name of the Son of God, so that you may know that you have eternal life.
>
> 1 John 5:13 HCSB

It is essential to understand that God is the one who saves us. He does the work. We do nothing.

This Biblical letter is a must-read for new Christians. John provides guidance, teaching, and illustrations that reassure us of our salvation. He teaches us that salvation is based on the objective truth of the Word of God and not on feelings.

> This is the way we know that we belong to the way of truth. When our hearts make us feel guilty, we can still have peace before God. God is greater than our hearts, and he knows everything.
>
> 1 John 3:20 NCV

Feeling convicted when you sin (do not follow God) indicates that you believe in God! Wanting to follow God is following God. If you wonder if you are saved, go back to God's objective truths. Did you call on God? Did you ask him to save you? Did you tell Jesus that you believed in him? If you did, you are saved regardless of your struggles or feelings at the moment. The truth is,

> ...Anyone who calls on the Lord will be saved.
>
> Romans 10:13 NCV

It is essential to understand that God is the one who saves us. He does the work. We do nothing. Salvation is a gift given to anyone who believes, calls on the name of the Lord, and declares Jesus as Lord.

> If you openly declare that Jesus is Lord and believe in your heart that God raised him from the dead, you will be saved. For it is by believing in your heart that you are made right with God, and it is by openly declaring your faith that you are saved.
>
> Romans 10:9-10

1 What two things happened when you believed and declared Jesus as Lord?

_____

_____

According to God's Word, his objective truth, you were made right with God and saved. God no longer sees you as a sinner. You are part of his family. He has settled any differences, forgiven your sins, and adopted you. Your relationship with him has changed into a good relationship. Being made right and being saved are things that God does, not things you do. Again, if you call on the name of the Lord, you are saved. That is the objective truth.

WILL GOD OR CAN SOMEONE TAKE MY SALVATION?

Day 2

Not only has God saved you, but according to Jesus, he will not lose you.

> However, those the Father has given me will come to me, and I will never reject them. For I have come down from heaven to do the will of God who sent me, not to do my own will. And this is the will of God, that I should not lose even one of all those he has given me, but that I should raise them up at the last day. For it is my Father's will that all who see his Son and believe in him should have eternal life. I will raise them up at the last day."
>
> John 6:37 NLT

Jesus Christ promises that he will not cast you out of the family. It is God's will that Jesus does not lose one single Christian along the way. He will be there with you until the end, and he will keep raising you up. Jesus also said no one can take you away from him.

> My sheep listen to my voice; I know them, and they follow me. I give them eternal life, and they will never perish. No one can snatch them away from me, for my Father has given them to me, and he is more powerful than anyone else. No one can snatch them from the Father's hand.
>
> John 10:27-29 NLT

QUICK, SMART START

God's will is that Jesus will not lose one single believer. He promises that no one can snatch you away from him. Jesus is powerful enough to ensure that promise. Jesus is committed to your new relationship. So committed that he has already given you eternal life. Yes, your eternal life began the moment you were saved.

❷ Before you move forward in this week's study, answer this question. Do you remember your moment of salvation? Describe it in the space below.

_____

_____

_____

_____

_____

If you cannot remember that moment, take a few minutes before moving on and ask yourself, "Do I believe in Jesus?" If you believe, make this moment the moment of your salvation. Make this moment the beginning of your new eternity.

Ask Jesus to forgive you. Ask God to save you. Ask God to have his Holy Spirit live in you and guide you. And finish the task, call someone and tell them that Jesus is Lord of your life!

❸ If you just asked God to save you, who did you tell? What was their reaction?

_____

_____

If you were saved before you started this study, how did you tell the world?

_____

_____

If your experience is like most, one of two things happened when you told people that you got saved. They were excited or looked at you like they did not know what to do. Other believers are usually excited when they hear about someone getting saved. Unbelievers have no idea what to do when they hear that someone has become a believer. They have no context to grasp what happened in your world. They might ask questions. They will definitely be watching as your new life unfolds. You have an excellent opportunity to share with them what you are experiencing. Maybe, just maybe, they will start their new eternity too.

When you are struggling and do not feel very "Christian," remember the facts of your salvation. God loves you. God is the one who invited you to follow. When you asked, God did the work. He made you right. And Jesus is God. Jesus saved you, and he will not lose you.

❺ Take a minute to review your memory verse for this week. Write it below.

_____

_____

_____

Years ago, I was on vacation with my extended family in Hilton Head, South Carolina. Three of us boys got bored, and I convinced Mike (my teenage brother-in-law) and his friend, Eric, to go sailing. As we sailed faster and faster, my hat (a gift from my father, who was one of my heroes) blew off into the sea. Without thinking, I jumped off the boat. I got my hat, but then the unexpected happened. I turned to go back to the boat only to find it was several football fields away and still moving. I panicked. What was I thinking? I was in over my head without a lifejacket, treading water, and holding a hat that might be my death. What I have not told you is that Mike and Eric did not know how to sail. They kept trying to get back to me but only zoomed by, never close enough. My lifeguard training kept telling me not to panic, but fear gripped me more each moment. I have never been so scared or felt so helpless. Finally, as the boat got near, Eric, now wearing a lifejacket, jumped off, holding a life jacket for me. What a risk, even with a lifejacket.

Eric jumped off that boat without a thought for his own safety and became my savior. Mike eventually got close and dropped the sail. Boy, was I embarrassed as Eric and I climbed on the boat. Eric was such a hero jumping off the boat and putting himself at risk to rescue me from my thoughtless act. That is what Jesus did for you. He saw your distress and need and jumped off the boat to save you when you were a mess, in a mess, and by most people's thinking, not worth it. Neither Eric nor Jesus were concerned with my error. They were concerned with my salvation. The truth is that they saved me in my error from the consequences of my error.

QUICK, SMART START

CAN I DO SOMETHING TO LOSE MY SALVATION?

You know that no one can take away the salvation that God has given you. No one can snatch you out of God's hand. You know that God is not going to take away your salvation. He does not intend and will not lose you from His family. But can you do something that will cause you to get booted out of God's family?

The answer is a simple, "No."

❻ Read the Romans 8:38-39 verse and answer the following questions.

> For I am sure that neither death nor life, nor angels nor rulers, nor things present nor things to come, nor powers, 39nor height nor depth, nor anything else in all creation, will be able to separate us from the love of God in Christ Jesus our Lord.
> Romans 8:38-39

What cannot separate you from God and His love for you?

_____

_____

Can any human separate you from God?

_____

_____

Are you human?

_____

_____

Paul taught an incredible truth to the Roman believers about eternal security. Nothing spiritual, no leader, no human, nothing can separate us from God's love. Jesus saved us, and no one is going to change that fact. Not even you or your actions (nothing) can separate you from God.

Paul cleared this up for the believers in Ephesus when he reminded them that salvation was a gift.

> God saved you by his grace when you believed. And you can't take credit for this; it is a gift from God. Salvation is not a reward for the good things we have done, so none of us can boast about it.
>
> Ephesians 2:8-9 NLT

God saved us by his choice, not as a reward for our actions. No man can lose his salvation because no man earned his salvation. When we ask, "Can I lose my salvation?" we assume that salvation is based on something we did or some value we have to God. We think that if our value declines, we could lose our salvation. We are assuming that we did something to be saved. Nothing could be further from the truth.

Paul shares this incredible truth in Romans 5:8-11,

> But God showed his great love for us by sending Christ to die for us while we were still sinners. And since we have been made right in God's sight by the blood of Christ, he will certainly save us from God's condemnation. For since our friendship with God was restored by the death of his Son while we were still his enemies, we will certainly be saved through the life of his Son. So now we can rejoice in our wonderful new relationship with God because our Lord Jesus Christ has made us friends of God.
>
> Romans 5:8-11 NLT

We were not good enough when God saved us (see **Romans 3:23**). His standard for our performance was low. He did not save us because we deserved it. He saved us because he us. Salvation is a free gift to his children who in no way deserve it.

> For the wages of sin is death, but the free gift of God is eternal life through Christ Jesus our Lord.
>
> Romans 6:23 NASB

None of us can sink lower than we were on the day we were saved. Just like Eric rescued me in the middle of my error, God rescued us in the middle of our errors. Your relationship with God is now a good father to

Romans 3:23

For everyone has sinned; we all fall short of God's glorious standard.

Ephesians 1:13-14

In him you also, when you heard the word of truth, the gospel of your salvation, and believed in him, were sealed with the promised Holy Spirit, who is the guarantee of our inheritance until we acquire possession of it, to the praise of his glory. ESV

a loved child by a spiritual birth. When you were born physically, there was a record made of your birth called a birth certificate. Your birth certificate was marked with a seal. When you were born again, a record was made in heaven. (see 1 John 5:11-13, Revelation 20:11-15). You are God's child, and the Holy Spirit has sealed your spiritual birth certificate.

In Jesus' day, authorities had a stamp, a seal, that they put on documents and proclamations. The seal verified that the ruler or owner had executed this agreement or declaration. In those days, when a ruler put his seal on something, not even he could revoke the order - it was a done deal.

 Read Ephesians 1:13-14, 4:30 in the column and answer the following questions.

Who guarantees your inheritance (salvation and eternal life)?

_____

What did you do to get that guarantee?

_____

Ephesians 4:30

And do not bring sorrow to God's Holy Spirit by the way you live. Remember he has identified you as his own, guaranteeing that you will be saved on the day of redemption.

What is your inheritance?

_____

God guarantees our inheritance of eternal life. He is our Father, and he has promised us an inheritance from him - eternal life in heaven. God's guarantee lasts until we get to heaven. The only thing we did to receive this inheritance was to believe. Paul used the language of his time when he used the word "sealed." He was making his point clear: your salvation was sealed with the Holy Spirit (the Spirit that is inside you). It is a done deal. Your salvation will never be revoked.

You will be your earthly father's child for eternity because you were born into that family. You can leave the country, disown each other, change your name, and never see him for the rest of your life, but it does not change the fact that your earthly father is your father. The same is true of your Heavenly Father. You cannot be unborn. Your birth is fixed forever, both physically and spiritually. Even God Himself cannot change that fact.

CAN I DO WHATEVER I WANT?

If your salvation is sealed, if you cannot lose it, can you do whatever you want? Technically speaking, if you are a believer, you can do whatever you want (sin) and still be God's child.

Jesus told a parable about a son that demanded his inheritance long before his father died. He wanted his freedom. He wanted to take his inheritance and do whatever he wanted. His father allowed him to go, but the father never ever questioned whether his rebellious son was his son. In fact, every day, the father looked down the road to see if his son was coming home. The son went off and wasted his inheritance doing what he pleased until he was broke. Even then, his pride kept him from returning home. He got so poor that he became a menial worker sharing food with the animals he cared for. One day he decided that if he was going to be a servant, he might as well be a servant for his father. He headed home to find his father waiting, then running down the road proclaiming, "My son that was lost is home!"

The point of the parable is that once you are born into the family of God, he is always your father. Even if you wander off.

So the question remains, "Can you do whatever you want?" Technically the answer is "yes," but a better question is, "Why would you?" Henry Blackaby is quoted as saying,

> If you have an obedience problem, you have a love problem.

If you really understand your salvation, believe in God, and love him, why would you ignore his life-giving truths that lead you to an abundant life? Paul addressed this when teaching the Roman believers.

8 Read Romans 6:1-14 and answer the following:

Verse 1 - Should we keep on sinning?

_____

Verse 6 - What happened to our old life?

_____

Verse 4 - What happened when we were baptized into Christ?

_____

Verse 4 - What is symbolized when we come up out of the water of baptism?

Our love for God is shown by us following him.

_____

Verse 7 - Does sin control us?

_____

Verse 11 - What makes us truly alive?

_____

Verse 13 - Who should we offer ourselves to?

_____

Our old life died when we became Christians. God gave us a new life. We died to our old selves, and Christ raised us up new. Sin is no longer our master. Believers have a new life and a new Master to follow - Jesus. Jesus put it this way.

> Those who accept my commandments and obey them are the ones who love me. And because they love me, my Father will love them. And I will love them and reveal myself to each of them.
>
> John 14:21

James put it simply,

> So you see, faith by itself isn't enough. Unless it produces good deeds, it is dead and useless. 18Now someone may argue, "Some people have faith; others have good deeds." But I say, "How can you show me your faith if you don't have good deeds? I will show you my faith by my good deeds."
>
> James 2:17-18

Our love for God is shown by us following him. Sin will not cause you to lose your salvation, but it will mess up your relationship. Disobedience has consequences. God will discipline us when we disobey. If you have an enduring sin problem, you may need to step back and ask, "Do I really believe that Jesus is Lord, ruler of all, savior of all?"

Disciples follow Christ's teaching because they are followers. Followers follow because they want to be like their incredible Savior. Why would any of us ever want to shame the Savior who loves us? Why would we ignore the very one we have chosen to follow?

9 Take a minute and write out your memory verse.

_____

_____

_____

10 In your own words, what is the purpose of this lesson?

_____

_____

_____

AT THE END OF THE WEEK ANSWER THESE QUESTIONS

What was the most meaningful statement(s) or scripture this week?	Reword the statement or scripture into a prayer of response to God.	What actions do you need to take in response to this week's study?
_____	_____	_____
_____	_____	_____
_____	_____	_____
_____	_____	_____
_____	_____	_____

TRUTH 3

MEMORY VERSE

Peter said to them, "Repent, and each of you be baptized in the name of Jesus Christ for the forgiveness of your sins; and you will receive the gift of the Holy Spirit."

Acts 2:38 NASB

What is Baptism?

Why Should I Be Baptized?

If you just became a Christian, you might wonder why anyone would ask this question. I joined God's family in my mid-twenties. I remember the moment and the days following. I was new. I felt clean. God forgave me, and I had a new life to live. I could not wait to be baptized. My excitement was impossible to contain.

But I had no idea why I was getting baptized. I was just doing what I was told, following my new leaders, doing what I had seen others do. And honestly, nothing really felt different after my baptism. My leaders explained the idea of baptism to me, but I was entirely overwhelmed with new information. It wasn't until years later that I actually understood baptism. Your experience might be the same as mine.

But, different organizations do things in different ways. The folks who helped me find Christ only baptized people who were saved. But many churches baptize infants and children. If that is your experience, you might wonder, "Why should I be baptized? I was baptized as a child."

Regardless of your experience, knowing what baptism is and why you should be baptized is important. There is a lot of important information about your salvation wrapped up in this first simple step of obedience. I wish I knew earlier all that I know today. I hope the truth about baptism helps you toward your next step as you grow.

QUICK, SMART START

WHAT IS BAPTISM?

Words become defined and redefined by culture, practice, and life. There are many definitions of "baptism" specific to different cultures and religions. Even Christians have several definitions based on their personal beliefs and practices. But, the oldest descriptions of baptism are:

> Baptism is being covered wholly with a fluid, to immerse, to submerge, or as in Old English "to make whelmed" (fully wet).

Followers of God have always practiced baptism. Long before Christianity, the Israelites (our Old Testament, spiritual forefathers) practiced baptism. In the Old Testament, baptism was primarily for repentance as they acknowledged their sin and turned back to right living. The participant was symbolically washed from his wrongs and ready to walk with God again. This is the first type of baptism you will see in the Bible. It is also the first type of baptism you find in the New Testament (after Jesus was on the scene).

John (aka John the Baptist) was called by God to announce that Jesus was coming. He baptized people who were convicted of their wrongs and wanted to be ready for the coming Savior of the World. John baptized people the Hebrew way before they met Jesus. This is how he explained it:

> As for me, I baptize you with water for repentance, but He who is coming after me is mightier than I, and I am not fit to remove His sandals; He will baptize you with the Holy Spirit and fire.
> Matthew 3:11 NASB

Acts 2:1-3

On the day of Pentecost all the believers were meeting together in one place. Suddenly, there was a sound from heaven like the roaring of a mighty windstorm, and it filled the house where they were sitting. Then, what looked like flames or tongues of fire appeared and settled on each of them.

John's word picture was compelling. He was preparing the way for people to return to God by believing in Jesus. John was calling them back to the Father's promise that he would send his Son to save the world. John baptized for repentance (or return) but he spoke of the baptism that Jesus would perform: a baptism with the Holy Spirt and fire. When people become followers, Jesus gives them (immerses them in) the Holy Spirit. John's baptism was physical. Jesus' baptism is spiritual. When John wrote about fire baptism he was prophetically speaking of the first time believers would receive the Holy Spirit (see **Acts 2:1-3**).

WHAT IS BAPTISM?

❶ Take a minute to review your memory verse for this week. Write it below.

_____

_____

_____

The New Testament also introduced another type of baptism - believer's baptism. Believer's baptism is a person getting baptized after they become Christians. It is,

- a testimony of believing in the Good News of Christ,
- a testimony of joining the Christians (the family of God), and
- a picture of what happened spiritually when people believed in God.

When people become followers, Jesus gives them the Holy Spirit. Water baptism is physical. Jesus' baptism is spiritual.

The purpose of believers' baptism can be seen in Romans 6:1-4.

> What should we say then? Should we continue in sin in order that grace may multiply? Absolutely not! How can we who died to sin still live in it? Or are you unaware that all of us who were baptized into Christ Jesus were baptized into His death? Therefore we were buried with Him by baptism into death, in order that, just as Christ was raised from the dead by the glory of the Father, so we too may walk in a new way of life.
>
> Romans 6:1-4 HCSB

Paul was speaking of the spiritual baptism of Jesus and the picture of the believer's baptism. Believer's baptism symbolizes the death, burial, and resurrection of Jesus Christ. It symbolizes the believer dying to himself, being washed from his sins, and being reborn to a new spiritual life. Believers' baptism is a picture of our spiritual baptism into Christ. It identifies you with Jesus and is a public statement of your belief in God.

One of Jesus' first followers was a man named Peter. He spent three years with Jesus, and during that time, Peter became a believer. He was one of the first people to receive the Holy Spirit. Immediately after Jesus gave him the Holy Spirit, Peter preached to a large crowd telling them how they could know God and receive salvation. The people asked, "What must we do to be saved?" Peter replied,

QUICK, SMART START

"Repent, and each of you be baptized in the name of Jesus Christ for the forgiveness of your sins; and you will receive the gift of the Holy Spirit."

Acts 2:38 NASB

You can see the influence of Peter's experience. He knew that God would not only save people, he would also give them (or, baptize them in) the Holy Spirit. The baptism he commanded them to do was believer's baptism in water.

Acts 8:12

But now the people believed Philip's message of Good News concerning the Kingdom of God and the name of Jesus Christ. As a result, many men and women were baptized.

❷ Can you identify all three types of baptism in Acts 2:38?

_____

_____

_____

The three types of baptism are baptism of repentance, spiritual baptism, and believer's baptism.

Acts 9:17-18

So Ananias went and found Saul. He laid his hands on him and said, "Brother Saul, the Lord Jesus, who appeared to you on the road, has sent me so that you might regain your sight and be filled with the Holy Spirit." Instantly something like scales fell from Saul's eyes, and he regained his sight. Then he got up and was baptized.

❸ Why does God instruct believers to be baptized?

_____

_____

_____

DO I HAVE TO BE BAPTIZED TO BE SAVED?

Throughout the New Testament, you can find example after example of believer's baptism (see **Acts 8:12**, **Acts 2:41**, **Acts 9:17-18**, **Acts 16:30-33**). Jesus' own instructions highlight the importance of baptism in our spiritual journey.

> Go into all the world and preach the Good News to everyone. Anyone who believes and is baptized will be saved. But anyone who refuses to believe will be condemned.
>
> Mark 16:15-16

4 What did all the New Testament believers do after they were saved?

_____

_____

5 Why did they do what they did?

_____

_____

Jesus expected that those who called on His Name for salvation would be physically baptized as an outward symbol of a spiritual reality. Baptism is important. But baptism is not salvation and salvation is not baptism. Baptism does not save you. You believe in Jesus (get saved) and then you get baptized. A quick look at Ephesians 2:8-9 makes it clear. People are saved by grace through faith, not by their actions — even if that action is baptism.

> God saved you by his grace when you believed. And you can't take credit for this; it is a gift from God. Salvation is not a reward for the good things we have done, so none of us can boast about it.
>
> Ephesians 2:8-9 NLT

Acts 2:41 NASB

So then, those who had received his word were baptized; and that day there were added about three thousand souls.

Acts 16:30-33

"Sirs, what must I do to be saved?" They replied, "Believe in the Lord Jesus and you will be saved, along with everyone in your household." And they shared the word of the Lord with him and with all who lived in his household...Then he and everyone in his household were immediately baptized.

Church leaders often argue back and forth about whether a person needs to be baptized to be saved. But their arguments do not apply if you read God's words about salvation.

> **Romans 10:9-10**
>
> If you openly declare that Jesus is Lord and believe in your heart that God raised him from the dead, you will be saved. For it is by believing in your heart that you are made right with God, and it is by openly declaring your faith that you are saved.

- Your belief in God requires faith, and that faith comes from God. You do not do anything to be saved except believe (Ephesians 2:8-9).
- If you believe and confess your belief, you will be saved (**Romans 10:9-10**).
- If you call upon the name of the Lord you will be saved (Romans 10:13).
- If you become a Christian, you should be baptized (Acts 2:38).

Baptism is an important confession and public display of your decision to give up your old life and follow Jesus. Do you see it? If we apply God's truths, we will get baptized when we become followers. It is simple. Believe and be baptized, and there is no need to argue, question, or wonder.

❻ Why did you choose to be baptized?

_____
_____
_____
_____
_____

If your church holds a particular belief that baptism is required for salvation, respect your leaders. If you have questions after reading this book, investigate what the Bible has to say about baptism. God can teach you through his words. Whatever you do, do not get involved in educational arguments that separate Christians (see 2 Timothy 2:23-24).

THREE QUICK BAPTISM QUESTIONS

Who can be baptized?

The most comprehensive record of an individual's baptism is found in the book of Acts. Philip (an early and devoted follower) shared the good news of salvation with an Ethiopian official. As Phillip explained Jesus, the Ethiopian became a Christian and asked,

> Look! Water! What prevents me from being baptized?
> Acts 8:36 NASB

Philip must have said something about baptism as he told the Ethiopian how to get saved. Perhaps the Ethiopian asked, "What must I do to be saved?" and Philip used Peter's words, "Believe and be baptized!" Regardless, the Ethiopian believed and asked if he could be baptized. Philip replied,

> "If you believe with all your heart, you may." And he answered and said, "I believe that Jesus Christ is the Son of God." And he ordered the chariot to stop; and they both went down into the water, Philip as well as the eunuch, and he baptized him.
> Acts 8:37-38 NASB

The only requirements for becoming a Christian (see **Romans 10:9-10**) are the only requirements for believer's baptism:

- The belief that Jesus is Lord and Savior, and
- a confession that God raised Jesus from the dead.

The Ethiopian believed, and Phillip baptized him. Anyone who believes in Jesus and confesses that Jesus rose from the dead becomes a Christian. Anyone who calls on the name of the Lord will be saved. And, anyone who becomes a Christian can be baptized.

QUICK, SMART START

7 Have you experienced baptism as a believer? If not, the time is now. Talk to the person who led you to Christ and ask when you can be baptized! If you have experienced believer's baptism, take a minute to describe your experience. Did your experience line up with what you have been learning from the Bible? Write your answer on the lines below.

_____

_____

_____

_____

Leverage the opportunity of your baptism to invite as many unbelievers as possible so they will hear the good news.

Where should I be baptized?

The first Christians were baptized in public areas full of unbelievers. These baptisms led to other people hearing about God. Today, most baptisms are done in churches and only attended by those who already believe. The actual place of baptism is not too important. Your testimony is the vital point.

Baptism is a public confession of your faith in Jesus Christ. It only makes sense that you should be baptized in public, at least in front of your church family. Leverage the opportunity of your baptism to invite as many unbelievers as possible so they will hear the good news.

8 Where were you or where will you get baptized? How could you or can you leverage your baptism to tell others about your new life and how they can know God?

_____

_____

_____

_____

What about being baptized a second time?

You never need to be baptized again. But, you will encounter people being baptized for the second or, maybe even, a third time. Most of those repeat baptisms are like the baptisms for repentance in the Old Testament. People are getting baptized again to show a recommitment of their faith.

Do you need to be baptized each time you recommit? No. Your baptism was a statement of salvation to the world that does not need to be repeated.

9 Take a minute and write out your memory verse.

_____

_____

_____

10 In your own words, what is the purpose of this lesson?

_____

_____

_____

AT THE END OF THE WEEK ANSWER THESE QUESTIONS

What was the most meaningful statement(s) or scripture this week?	Reword the statement or scripture into a prayer of response to God.	What actions do you need to take in response to this week's study?

TRUTH 4

MEMORY VERSE

All Scripture is inspired by God and is useful to teach us what is true and to make us realize what is wrong in our lives. It corrects us when we are wrong and teaches us to do what is right. God uses it to prepare and equip his people to do every good work.

2 Timothy 3:16-17

The Bible

Eight Weeks that Changed My Life Forever

I was in my early thirties the first time I read my Bible cover-to-cover. I am not sure why I decided to read it in eight weeks, but I did. And I had no idea how much those eight weeks would change my life. I learned more useful truths in those eight weeks than I had learned from countless books, Bible studies, and Sundays.

It was like seeing the story of God all at once. Instead of studying one piece at a time, disconnected, I saw God's entire story in context. The beginning of humankind's walk on earth and their walk away from God in Genesis flowed easily into the second book, Exodus, where God rescued His people and made them into a nation. The words of the prophets in Isaiah, Jeremiah, Daniel, and Lamentations were like flashback pictures in a movie showing how the Israelites ended up losing their nation. The villains, the heroes, and the turning points of God and his people became evident. The need for Jesus' complete forgiveness began to make more sense.

The Holy Spirit would remind me of truths I read in the year that followed. My decisions began to be fueled by his truths. My life improved. I began to understand my humanity as I read countless stories of people struggling with pride, money, insecurity, and every kind of sin.

My second reading brought more power to my faith too. None of my highlights had anything to do with history, Greek, maps, deeper truths, theology, or what the length of a cubit was in inches. Those things may be interesting, but none helped me live my faith. As for the incredible, useful truths, I wondered, "Why didn't anyone teach me these truths? Why didn't they make God this simple?" I had tried things my way before I got saved. Now I was applying God's truths and seeing more success than ever. It was like I was becoming smarter. My life was becoming proof of what I read. God's design for life and humans was working for me. The Holy Spirit fueled better decisions for me and helpful moments for others. I traded guessing for confidence and surety. Christianity was finally working for me.

43

QUICK, SMART START

WHAT IS THE BIBLE?

As a friend of mine was teaching a crowd about Jesus, he held his Bible and said,

> The first few pages of the Bible record humans living with God in a perfect relationship. The last few pages tell of a future when that perfect lifestyle will be restored. The fifteen hundred pages in the middle are the history of people of God struggling with life and God trying to show them the way home.

Another friend says the Bible is the Basic Instructions Before Leaving Earth (B.I.B.L.E - cute, huh?) No matter how you describe it, the Bible continues to play an essential role in our lives.

The Bible is the most published, most translated book in the world. It focuses on the interactions of God and humankind over four thousand years. Its historical record is accurate. Its timeline is consistent with secular history. And the Bible continues to influence the ongoing actions of humankind. It's prophecies continue to be fulfilled, further validating its content. It's truths continue to show themselves everlasting. It's seemingly unbelievable miracles continue to be proven by archaeological discoveries. The Bible is so much more than a history book. It contains the words of God leading men and women to discover the one true living God. Its record reveals God's character, values, and love for his creation.

The Bible is a collection of sixty-six writings (called books) divided into two sections.

- The Old Testament is a collection of thirty-nine books recording the history of man and God from creation to Jesus' birth.
- The New Testament is a collection of twenty-seven books recording the history of man and God from Jesus' birth to the beginnings of Christianity.

The Bible was written by men inspired by God to record God's words and the history of God's followers. The Old Testament records the words of God spoken through angels and Spirit-filled prophets. It also records words spoken directly to men and women throughout history. The Old

Testament is full of God's instructions for living well and the successes and failures of those who learned to follow Him.

The New Testament records the eyewitness history of Jesus' life and what he taught while he was on earth. It documents the beginnings of the Church and Christianity. And it contains the teachings of the first disciples as they passed on Jesus' teaching. Throughout the Bible, you discover what God values and why he values it. You find useful principles you can use immediately to draw closer to God and live well.

The Bible is like a shortcut, a roadmap. It fuels your faith as you see God provide for people throughout history. It gives hope as you learn what God promises to those who follow Him. The Bible is amazing. God can speak directly to you in prayer, but there is so much that God has already spoken and longs for you to read. The Bible is a "how-to" manual for knowing God and living a great life.

1 Take a minute to review your memory verse for this week. Write it below.

_____

_____

_____

_____

WHAT IS THE PURPOSE OF THE BIBLE?

Day 2

The Bible records the bad times and the good times, the errors and the successes of humans following God. In its brutal honesty, we see how love has worked throughout history. We see how self-centeredness has never worked out well. We discover what is important to God and what breaks the beauty of his creation.

Those that followed God documented their experiences with God for future generations. Inspired by God, they recorded his words revealing who he is, his plans, and what is important to him. They documented his desires and direction for us to live an incredible life with him.

The writers were passing on the words spoken, the truths taught to them, and the wisdom the Spirit gave them. The Bible allows us to learn who God is, what he values, and what he desires. It contains words of correction and real-life examples of how people got it and missed it. It has his commands for following him. The Bible contains His words not only to his people but to a world that he longs to see reconciled to him.

God has never stopped calling people home, calling them back to belief in him. He has never stopped calling us to follow him into a life of love and prosperity. So the Bible is not only good for those who believe; it is a word of hope for those who do not yet believe.

4 Purposes for Those Who Do Not Believe

The Bible introduces readers to God. It demonstrates that God is the one, true living God who loves his creation and all people. Cover-to-cover, God shows his love. Cover-to-cover, God calls people to believe in Him and lays out a pathway for people to return to their Maker. Cover-to-cover, God reveals himself. When Paul wrote,

> You have been taught the holy Scriptures from childhood, and they have given you the wisdom to receive the salvation that comes by trusting in Christ Jesus.
>
> 2 Timothy 3:15

he reminded this young leader that the history and truths in the Bible were the very things that allowed him to believe in Jesus. In other words, **the Bible presents truths that bring us to salvation.**

❷ Take a moment and think about how you became a Christian. Who told you the truth? Where did that truth come from?

_____

_____

_____

_____

There is no doubt that they shared truths about God, Jesus, sin, salvation, and hope from the Bible. The Bible tells us how to know God

Romans 3:23

For everyone has sinned; we all fall short of God's glorious standard.

Romans 6:23

For the wages of sin is death, but the free gift of God is eternal life through Christ Jesus our Lord.

and find forgiveness. God uses the truths in the Bible to convict us of a better way as he brings the printed words to life, drawing a sharp line between right and wrong.

> For the word of God is alive and powerful. It is sharper than the sharpest two-edged sword, cutting between soul and spirit, between joint and marrow. It exposes our innermost thoughts and desires. Nothing in all creation is hidden from God. Everything is naked and exposed before his eyes, and he is the one to whom we are accountable.
>
> Hebrews 4:12-13

Romans 5:8

But God showed his great love for us by sending Christ to die for us while we were still sinners.

Do you see it? The Holy Spirit used the Word of God as fuel. When you were not following God (lost), the Spirit made God's words powerful, convincing you that you had sinned and needed forgiveness. He will use His Word for this exact purpose in others. **God convicts people of their need for him with His Word.**

 Take a moment and remember how you knew you were wrong, alone, and needed God. Write your answer below.

_____

_____

Romans 10:9-10,13

If you openly declare that Jesus is Lord and believe in your heart that God raised him from the dead, you will be saved. For it is by believing in your heart that you are made right with God, and it is by openly declaring your faith that you are saved. For "Everyone who calls on the name of the Lord will be saved."

I hope your answer was that God's words began to show you that you had sinned and that there was a better way. Perhaps someone shared the classic verses called the Romans Road to Salvation (see **Romans 3:23, 6:23, 5:8, and 10:9-10,13**), or perhaps they shared a scripture that specifically challenged your decisions or actions. Either way, every person who was or will ever believe in God finds God in the same way. Do you remember how we are saved?

> For by grace are you saved through faith...
>
> Ephesians 2:8-9 NASB

We are saved not by our works or anything we do. We are saved because we believe through faith. Now, look at where that faith comes from.

> So faith comes from hearing, and hearing by the word of Christ.
>
> Romans 10:17 NASB

QUICK, SMART START

The Bible is the foundation of our faith, our hope. And James tells us,

> So get rid of all the filth and evil in your lives, and humbly accept the word God has planted in your hearts, for it has the power to save your souls.
>
> James 1:21

Romans 1:16

For I am not ashamed of the gospel, for it is the power of God for salvation to everyone who believes, to the Jew first and also to the Greek.

God's Word is active in salvation. **The Bible has the power to save** (see **Romans 1:16**). Faith comes alive when people hear the Words of God, and the Spirit brings those words to life. And faith is the only way to salvation. People believe in God because they hear about God. People know they need to ask for forgiveness because the living word convicts them of their sinful ways. The Bible tells the entire world of God's love, desires, and character. It tells of man's creation, how we departed from God, and how we can return to God. The Bible records the promises of God for those that follow him and provides the pathway to real hope. God's Words, written and spoken, show us God.

❹ What are the four purposes of the Bible for those who do not believe?

_____

_____

_____

_____

The Bible has the truths of God that allow unbelievers to know about God, Jesus, and salvation. The Holy Spirit using the Bible, has the power to convict unbelievers of wrong. The Word of God allows unbelievers to have faith in God. The Bible has a God-given power to save unbelievers.

❺ Take a minute to review your memory verse for this week.

_____

_____

_____

The Purpose for Believers

Since you were saved by the Word of God, it must be your absolute, infallible guide to tell you how to live. Think about it. Every major purchase (car, appliance, etc.) is accompanied by an owner's manual telling you how to operate it. The Bible is God's "owner's manual" for a follower's life. God did not save and call you to this new life without giving you clear, exact directions. One mighty man of God described the power of God's words this way,

> Your word is a lamp for my feet and a light on my path.
> Psalm 119:105 HCSB

6 **Your memory verse for this week illustrates six purposes of God's Word in our lives. Review the verse and list those six purposes below:**

_____

_____

_____

_____

_____

_____

God's word is not one person's take on God. The Bible contains the inspired words of God. In other words, the Holy Spirit moved in the writers' hearts and minds to have them write what God wanted to be written. And those inspired words show us what is true and what is wrong, correct us when we are wrong, teach us to do right, prepare us for good work, and equip us for good work. For example, 1 John 3:16-17 reads,

> We know what real love is because Jesus gave up his life for us. So we also ought to give up our lives for our brothers and sisters. If someone has enough money to live well and sees a brother or sister in need but shows no compassion—how can God's love be in that person?
> 1 John 3:16-17

> **2 Timothy 3:16-17**
>
> All Scripture is inspired by God and is useful to teach us what is true and to make us realize what is wrong in our lives. It corrects us when we are wrong and teaches us to do what is right. God uses it to prepare and equip his people to do every good work.

First, John reminds us of what is true. God loves us. We know real love because Jesus gave his life for us. Jesus' sacrifice paid the penalty for our sin and provided forgiveness. His love sacrifice allows us to experience God's love relationship. Then, John teaches us what Jesus taught him. We should follow in Jesus' footsteps and give up our lives to allow others to experience God's love. We should love one another. Then John gave us an example of God's love in action — if we have what another Christian needs, we should share God's blessing.

But there is more; God's words through John go on to show us what is wrong. It is not loving to have what a fellow Christian needs and not share it. When we read what is right and wrong and the Holy Spirit convicts us that we are wrong, God's word corrects us. As John shares God's truths, he is preparing us to be like Christ. He is equipping us to live in community with other believers.

You will see this pattern again and again in the Word of God. The truths contained in the history, the prophecies, the proverbs, and the words of Jesus prepare us to live right (see Proverbs 3:5-6). And the truths of the Bible protect us from error. Paul put it this way as he taught the church in Ephesus,

> Therefore, put on every piece of God's armor so you will be able to resist the enemy in the time of evil. Then after the battle you will still be standing firm. Stand your ground, putting on the belt of truth and the body armor of God's righteousness. For shoes, put on the peace that comes from the Good News so that you will be fully prepared. In addition to all of these, hold up the shield of faith to stop the fiery arrows of the devil. 17Put on salvation as your helmet, and take the sword of the Spirit, which is the word of God.
>
> Ephesians 6:13-18

All the armor comes from the Bible. We find God's truth in the Bible. We can live righteously because God has made us righteous and modeled what is right in the Bible. Peace comes from the Good News that we can find salvation and peace in God. The Good News is found in the Bible. Faith in God and his promises deflects untruths whispered by the enemy. Faith, of course, comes from knowing the words of God. And the words of God are recorded in the Bible. We are saved because of God's words. We have the Spirit because of our salvation. And the Spirit's weapon of choice to protect us is, you guessed it, the Bible.

The word of God is also:

- Your guidebook for your journey in life;

> Trust in the Lord with all your heart, and do not rely on your own understanding; think about Him in all your ways, and He will guide you on the right paths.
>
> Proverbs 3:5-6 HCSB

- Like spiritual food for you;

> I have not departed from his commands, but have treasured his words more than daily food.
>
> Job 23:12

> When I discovered your words, I devoured them. They are my joy and my heart's delight,
>
> Jeremiah 15:16

- And, a cleansing agent.

> How can a young man keep his way pure? By keeping Your word. I have sought You with all my heart; don't let me wander from Your commands. I have treasured Your word in my heart so that I may not sin against You.
>
> Psalm 119:9-11 HCSB

> You are already clean because of the word I have spoken to you.
>
> John 15:3 HCSB

God's words, held in the book we call the Bible, have guided followers for thousands of years. Originally, His words were spoken to men and women directly. Later, His words were recorded alongside the history of God and man. Consuming the Bible allows you to know as much as possible about God, man, living, and the best way to live.

HOW DO I UNDERSTAND THE BIBLE?

God can use pastors, teachers, small group leaders, and family to help you understand the Bible. You can read Bible studies prepared by trustworthy Christians. Inspiring books by Christian authors can help you understand Biblical topics. Ultimately though, it is God's Spirit that causes us to understand God's words. Jesus had this to say about how we learn and understand the words of God,

> But the Counselor, the Holy Spirit—the Father will send Him in My name—will teach you all things and remind you of everything I have told you.
>
> John 14:26 HCSB

The Spirit is the one who leads and guides you into all truth regardless of how you become aware of those truths. The Spirit is the one who connects the dots and makes what we learn real to us. Jesus taught,

> When the Spirit of truth comes, he will guide you into all truth. He will not speak on his own but will tell you what he has heard.
>
> John 16:13

You need to rely on the Holy Spirit as you read God's words. You need to listen to God. He will stir your heart to see new truths and understand old truths. He can also help you connect one Biblical truth with another to help you understand. This fancy term for this connection of truths is inductive study.

Inductive study confirms what you think one passage means by observing the same truth in other places in the Bible. Comparing truths throughout the Bible allows the Spirit to correct, confirm, and expand our understanding of God and his ways. It may sound complex, but if you pray, listen to God, and just read, the Holy Spirit will naturally do his part.

7 Think of a time when you were confused by something you read in the Bible and describe it below. What was your approach to solving the confusion?

_____

_____

_____

As you begin to read the Bible more, there will be times when it seems ridiculously repetitive. So often, it seems to be teaching the same truths, telling the same story, and giving the same instructions, again and again. Often, the repetition is exact. For example, God tells us again and again to take a day of rest. The Sabbath (a day of rest) is one of God's hottest topics. He even disciplines the nation of Israel for not allowing their fields to rest. Why does he repeat this simple truth again and again? Because God's people always struggle to follow the simple principle that all creation needs rest.

As you read the Bible cover-to-cover, you will see followers ignore rest, again and again. It feels repetitive because you are reading thousands of years of history compressed. In actuality, God is simply speaking the same truth to new generations. But, take note when you see truths repeated again and again. The Holy Spirit might warn you of a common error that challenges every follower. Listening might help you avoid that error. The Spirit might show you something that always brings success. Listening will help you repeat that success. Always take note when you see things repeated.

You will also see repetition as different writers record the same story. Some stories are told two, three, or even four times throughout the Bible. But, each redundancy comes with a different perspective and often an additional truth. What seems like needless repetition to us can actually provide a safety net as we learn about God.

Throughout the Bible, God's truths are consistent. A truth learned in one passage will never contradict another Biblical truth. Likewise, when we see the same truth repeatedly, it adds confidence to our understanding. Your role is to consume His words, listen to wise teachers, and verify what you are learning. Luke praises a group of believers for this type of learning.

Throughout the Bible, God's truths are consistent. A truth learned in one passage will never contradict another Biblical truth.

QUICK, SMART START

> And the people of Berea were more open-minded than those in Thessalonica, and they listened eagerly to Paul's message. They searched the Scriptures day after day to see if Paul and Silas were teaching the truth. As a result, many Jews believed, as did many of the prominent Greek women and men.
>
> Acts 17:11 NLT

Paul was thoroughly trained in the Old Testament before he became a Christian. God used that training to make Paul one of the leading teachers and scholars in the New Testament times. His insights were incredible. He was the godfather of most of our contemporary understanding of God and Jesus. The believers that lived in Berea listened to him, but they checked out what he taught. They took responsibility for making sure that their teacher was teaching the truth. They consumed God's words and listened to wise teachers. They also compared what Paul taught to everything God had already taught in the Bible. They listened to the teaching, fact-checked it, relied on the Spirit, and then applied the teaching to their lives. And their leaders praised them for it. Your role is to consume all God's words — relying on the Holy Spirit to connect and verify the truths you find.

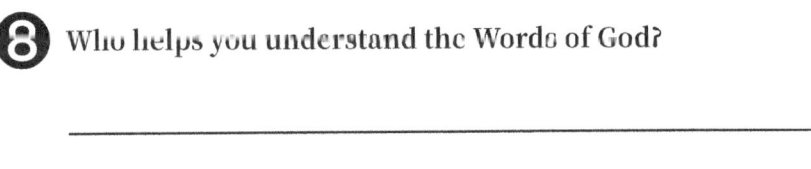

Who helps you understand the Words of God?

_____

_____

WHERE SHOULD I START READING?

If you are part of a Sustainable Discipleship group, you are already reading the Bible cover-to-cover. Stick with that plan - it works! But what about everyone else? How do you answer this question for the new believer who wants to get reading?

"Where should I start?" is a common question, and there are as many opinions as there are teachers. Most agree that starting with Chronicles, Numbers, Isaiah, or Jeremiah will be difficult. These books are loaded with genealogies, long histories, and complex prophecies. If you are just starting, finding useful truths in these books can be difficult. You might also avoid starting with Romans or Corinthians in the New Testament. Paul, the author, was an incredible scholar, but his writings can be challenging to understand at first. Peter, a contemporary of Paul's, said this about Paul's writing,

> And remember, our Lord's patience gives people time to be saved. This is what our beloved brother Paul also wrote to you with the wisdom God gave him— speaking of these things in all of his letters. Some of his comments are hard to understand, and those who are ignorant and unstable have twisted his letters to mean something quite different, just as they do with other parts of Scripture.
>
> 1 Peter 3:15-16

John 20:31

But these are written so that you may continue to believe that Jesus is the Messiah, the Son of God, and that by believing in him you will have life by the power of his name.

Peter understood God. He walked with Jesus. And even he recognized the difficulty of Paul's style. New Christians get excited about reading the end of the Bible, Revelation. It is full of mystery and fantastic foreshadowing about when Jesus returns to earth. No doubt, Revelation is an exciting read, but its prophecy is almost too great to understand. It can be a challenge for new readers to find truths that apply to their lives.

So, where do you start?

A solid choice is to start books in the Bible that are highly relevant to your relationship with God.

- Matthew, Mark, Luke, and John, called the "Gospels," share the Good News of Jesus (gospel means good news). These books record the life, the miracles, and the words of Jesus from his birth to his death. They provide an excellent opportunity to get to know Jesus.

- The Gospel of John was written to help people believe in the Lord Jesus Christ (see **John 20:31**).

- 1 John was written to help people know they are saved (see 1 John 5:13).

- Psalm 119 illustrates the value of the Word of God to us.

- James has short bits of practical wisdom to help us follow God and understand our faith.

- Proverbs is a collection of simple, one-liner truths that are easy to apply as you get started. This book is full of practical, useful wisdom on living.

- Peter is an excellent book for those figuring out how to live as a Christian in an unsaved world, with unsaved bosses, families, and friends.

It is incredible how much you can learn just by reading. You can read the Bible cover-to-cover in about seventy-six hours. That is a little more than three days or twelve minutes a day for a year. But, having a guide in the beginning, can also be helpful.

Understanding Biblical truths takes time. You will discover the need to differentiate historical records from God's direct instructions. Some stories will not make sense until translated into today's culture. It can be challenging to determine which truths apply to all believers and which are for specific people. No matter what, begin your lifelong process of understanding the Bible by reading it. Just read it and see what God has to say to you. Pray and listen to the Holy Spirit. Let him connect the dots. Find an experienced guide. Take your time.

9 Take a minute and write out your memory verse.

_____

_____

_____

10 In your own words, what is the purpose of this lesson?

_____

_____

_____

_____

AT THE END OF THE WEEK ANSWER THESE QUESTIONS

What was the most meaningful statement(s) or scripture this week?

_____
_____
_____
_____
_____
_____

Reword the statement or scripture into a prayer of response to God.

_____
_____
_____
_____
_____
_____

What actions do you need to take in response to this week's study?

_____
_____
_____
_____
_____
_____

TRUTH 5

MEMORY VERSE

So I say, let the Holy Spirit guide your lives. Then you won't be doing what your sinful nature craves.

Galatians 5:16

The Holy Spirit

I Really Needed to Stop Whining

I have a tendency to whine. It is kind of a thorn in the flesh, so to speak. And for years, I whined about not having someone to guide me in my early years of Christianity. Don't get me wrong - someone should have been there to point me to God, to disciple me. But as I look back, I had a guide. An excellent guide - the Holy Spirit. I just didn't recognize him.

We see God in three ways. He is one God, but he has shown up in the history of humankind in three ways: the Father, the Son, and the Holy Spirit.

- The Father guided his followers and sent the Son,
- The Son guided us back to God and sent the Holy Spirit, and
- The Holy Spirit guides us to live after we believe.

The Holy Spirit is a great guide. He doesn't just point the way. He walks with us along the way giving us real-time direction and inspiration. He helps carry the load when we are overwhelmed. That's right, he actually prays for us and our needs. He is a special guide because he provides transformation. He doesn't just tell us to be pure; he purifies us. He doesn't just tell us to be patient; he is a source of patience in us. The Holy Spirit does the work of God in us to give us the incredible character of Christ. All we have to do is listen, allow him to work, and follow His teaching. He is also a source of power, like energy to do things and a strength that can overcome the world, even sickness. The Holy Spirit is the power of God in me.

If you are a believer, you have that power too. You have a guide, the best guide that you could ever have. It took me a while to recognize him and to listen closely. Don't make that same mistake.

QUICK, SMART START

WHAT IS THE FUNCTION OF THE HOLY SPIRIT IN MY LIFE?

God has revealed himself to us as Father, Son, and Holy Spirit. It is easy to grasp the idea of God as our father because we all have fathers. It is easy to understand God as a son because we are children or have children. It is not so easy to understand God as the Holy Spirit because our only earthly concept of spirit is the idea of ghosts.

The Holy Spirit might be the most ignored and misunderstood part of a Christian's relationship with God. Some Christians have gone too far, trivializing and abusing the idea and gifts of the Spirit (you know, those swoopy-haired, showy preachers). Other believers avoid talking about the Holy Spirit. The Spirit seems too mystical to them. These believers are trying to stay "level-headed" and avoid craziness. You do not need to get obsessed with the mystery of the Holy Spirit, but you cannot ignore the Holy Spirit. To fully experience God, you must experience Him as Father, Son, and Holy Spirit.

Galatians 5:16

So I say, let the Holy Spirit guide your lives. Then you won't be doing what your sinful nature craves.

The Holy Spirit is where the mystical (the unseen and immaterial) connects with the practical (our lives as believers). You cannot understand the teachings of God without the Holy Spirit. You cannot hear from God without the Holy Spirit. You cannot receive God's spiritual gifts without the Holy Spirit. The Father sent the Son, Jesus, so we could have a relationship with God. Jesus showed us the way to God while he was on earth. He gave his life to pave that way and provide forgiveness for our sins. Then Jesus rose from the dead, defeating death and bringing new life to all who believe. When he rose from the dead, he went to heaven and sent us the gift of the Holy Spirit. The Holy Spirit is our connection to God that continues to teach, guide, and give us the power and ability to follow God. Yes, the Holy Spirit is mystical, but he accomplishes very practical things in our lives. The key to understanding the Spirit is balancing the mystical and the practical. You can find that balance with a Biblical understanding of the Holy Spirit of God and His role in your life.

❶ Take a minute to review your memory verse for this week. Write it below.

WHERE DO I FIND THE HOLY SPIRIT?

Day 2

You have a spirit — that immaterial part of you that is in your body. It is somewhere and everywhere in your body. We often call it our heart. The Bible refers to the location as the guts. Have you had that feeling deep inside your stomach when your spirit groans or rejoices?

When you became a Christian, God joined his Spirit (the Holy Spirit) to yours. Jesus explained it this way,

> "If you love me, you will obey my commandments. And I will ask the Father, and he will give you another Advocate, who will never leave you. He is the Holy Spirit who leads into all truth. The world cannot receive him because it isn't looking for him and doesn't recognize him. But you know him, because he lives with you now and later will be in you.
>
> John 14:17 NLT

❷ Who did Jesus promise to give to the believer?

_____

_____

Jesus promised to send the Holy Spirit. He made this promise to his followers before his death, burial, resurrection (coming back to life), and ascension (going to heaven). He taught them that the Spirit would live with them for the time being but that a day would come when the Spirit would live in them. And that day did come. After Jesus ascended to heaven, he sent his Spirit to dwell in the believers' hearts (see **Acts 2:1-4**). Since that time, the Spirit has always lived inside everyone who believes.

Paul reiterated this truth as he taught us to live well on this earth.

> Don't you realize that your body is the temple of the Holy Spirit, who lives in you and was given to you by God?
>
> 1 Corinthians 6:19 NLT

Acts 2:1-4

On the day of Pentecost all the believers were meeting together in one place. Suddenly, there was a sound from heaven like the roaring of a mighty windstorm, and it filled the house where they were sitting. Then, what looked like flames or tongues of fire appeared and settled on each of them. And everyone present was filled with the Holy Spirit…

> And because we are his children, God has sent the Spirit of his Son into our hearts, prompting us to call out, "Abba, Father."
>
> Galatians 4:6

John, who learned directly from Jesus, tells us,

> If anyone acknowledges that Jesus is the Son of God, God lives in them and they in God.
>
> 1 John 4:15 NIV

The Holy Spirit of God lives in and is inside each believer. It is a mystical but very practical truth. Jesus explained the mystery of God's unseen spirit to a prominent Jewish leader struggling to understand salvation. Here is what Jesus told him,

> Humans can reproduce only human life, but the Holy Spirit gives birth to spiritual life. So don't be surprised when I say, 'You must be born again.' The wind blows wherever it wants. Just as you can hear the wind but can't tell where it comes from or where it is going, so you can't explain how people are born of the Spirit.
>
> John 3:6-8

John 16:8

And when he comes, he will convict the world of its sin, and of God's righteousness, and of the coming judgment.

Like the wind, we may not be able to see the Holy Spirit. We may not be able to know its exact location. But, we can see the results of the Spirit like we see trees bending under the unseen wind. The Holy Spirit is inside your body. He is the power, the strength, and your direct connection to God. You will never see him, but, like the wind, you will hear the Spirit's voice and see His work in your life as you follow God.

❸ Have you ever sensed the presence of God? Have you "felt" his Spirit moving in you during worship or as you read an incredible God truth? What did it feel like?

_____

_____

_____

WHAT IS THE HOLY SPIRIT?

In his article, "Does the Holy Spirit Live in You?," Billy Graham beautifully and simply explained the Holy Spirit.

> The Holy Spirit is not an "it." The Holy Spirit is a Person. The Bible says that He is not something, He is Someone. He is God. There are three Persons in the Trinity–God the Father, God the Son, and God the Holy Spirit. The Bible teaches that the Holy Spirit is all-powerful. We read in Micah 3:8, "I am full of power by the Spirit of the Lord." The Bible says that God is present everywhere. No matter where we go, He is there. "Where can I go from Your Spirit? Or where can I flee from Your presence?" (Psalm 139:7). The Holy Spirit can be in both your heart and my heart, even though we may live a thousand miles apart. The Holy Spirit has all knowledge. The Bible says, "The Spirit searches all things, yes, the deep things of God" (1 Corinthians 2:10). It is the Holy Spirit who teaches us and takes us deeper and deeper into God's truth as we go along in our Christian life. We are to grow in the grace and knowledge of Christ, but we can grow only by the help of the Holy Spirit.

The Holy Spirit is God. He is one of the ways that God shows himself to people. The Spirit is not a what but a who.

WHAT DOES THE HOLY SPIRIT DO?

The Holy Spirit, God, communicates with us at our innermost being — our spirit. Before salvation, the Spirit convicts the lost of sin. He draws them to see God and to see their need for salvation (see John 16:8). After salvation, God's Spirit lives in us in an inexplicable, miraculous way accomplishing all sorts of incredible work.

Read each Bible verse below and describe the Holy Spirit's work.

- John 16:13

  _____

- John 14:26; 16:13-15; 1 Corinthians 2:9-10

  _____

- 1 Peter 1:2

  _____

- Galatians 5:22-24

  _____

- John 3:3-8

  _____

- Ephesians 1:13-14; 4:30

  _____

- Romans 8:26-27; Ephesians 2:18

  _____

- John 14:15-18; 2 Timothy 1:7

  _____

- Zechariah 4:6; Ephesians 3:16; 2 Corinthians 4:7

  _____

1 John 4:13; Romans 8:16

  _____

The Holy Spirit guides believers and teaches believers. He cleans us up and sets us apart for Him and good.

The Holy Spirit guides believers and teaches believers. He cleans us up and sets us apart for Him and good. He causes "spiritual fruit" to grow in our lives. The Holy Spirit creates, regenerates, and secures the saved. He prays for you, comforts you, and empowers you to serve God. He testifies that you are saved. All this work began in you the moment you became a Christian. Some of His work will happen quietly, often unnoticed in the background. Other parts of God's work will be very noticeable as the Holy Spirit begins to work and speak to our Spirit. The most immediate and noticeable work will be us becoming convicted of right and wrong.

WHAT IS CONVICTION?

Conviction is often confused with feeling guilty, but conviction in the Bible has nothing to do with our feelings. Conviction is more like becoming convinced. When God convicts us, we become convinced to adjust, convinced to act, convinced to change, convinced that we are right, convinced that we are wrong, and convinced that His truths are right for us.

Christians often speak of conviction only as God convincing us that we are wrong. It is easy to connect conviction to our judicial system, where people are judged, convicted, and suffer some kind of discipline. But the Holy Spirit's conviction is not always a negative thing. God convicts us to follow Him, convicts us of his truths, and so much more.

Notice how the Holy Spirit brought conviction (certainty) of the message of God:

> for our gospel did not come to you in word only, but also in power and in the Holy Spirit and with full conviction; just as you know what kind of men we proved to be among you for your sake.
>
> 1 Thessalonians 1:5 NASB

Conviction from the Holy Spirit is being confident that something is true even when you cannot see results. The writer of Hebrews teaches that faith in God is being confident that God is God even though you cannot see Him.

> Now faith is the assurance of things hoped for, the conviction of things not seen.
>
> Hebrews 11:1 NASB

Conviction is being sure of what you believe (or actually anything). The Holy Spirit convicts us of many things so that we can be prepared, confident, and ready to follow God. Whether he is convicting us of wrong or convicting us of what is right, His conviction is always for our good.

❺ Stop for a moment and sit quietly. What is the last thing that Holy Spirit convicted you was wrong, something that you needed to change? Write it below.

_____

_____

6 At that moment, did you also know what God wanted you to do instead of doing the thing that he did not want you to do? If so, write it below.

_____

7 Did you know why God wanted you to change?

_____

Sometimes, the Holy Spirit will convict us that we need to stop a behavior. But in most convictions, there is also a call to start something. God wants us to practice a good behavior for our own good, the good of others, or for the good of his mission on earth. When we become aware of the right thing, we also become aware of the wrong thing. God's desire for the right thing creates a conviction to stop the wrong thing. It is so important to understand that the Holy Spirit convinces us of what is good as well as of what is wrong.

Truth is what the Holy Spirit uses to convict us. He uses God's eternal truths. There are times when God, through His Holy Spirit connection with you, will say, "You need to stop." But most of the time, when the Holy Spirit convinces us to stop something, it is because he wants us to start something.

Day 6: WHAT IS THE DIFFERENCE BETWEEN CONVICTION AND GUILT?

Many believers confuse conviction with feeling guilt or shame. Conviction is God telling you something needs to change. Guilt is feeling bad about what you have or have not done.

Conviction is a factual judgment of our actions by the Spirit. It is not a feeling. Conviction is the Holy Spirit saying deep within, "You need to change. Do this (or don't do that)." For example, if you realize you took a pencil from work, the Spirit might remind you of the verse "do not steal." This is the conviction of wrong. The Spirit might convict you to take time to read God's Word. He might remind you of the verse "all Scripture is inspired and good for us." This is conviction of something God wants you to do.

The proper response to the conviction of wrong is to make it right. You return that pencil. You ask a person you hurt to forgive you. You confess your error to God, who restores you. God used a prophet to convict his people of their wrong and then said to them,

> Come now, let's settle this," says the Lord. "Though your sins are like scarlet, I will make them as white as snow. Though they are red like crimson, I will make them as white as wool.
>
> Isaiah 1:18

The proper response to the conviction to do something good is to do it. You read that Bible. You stop to help a stranger. You take more time to talk to God.

Guilt is much different than conviction. Guilt is what we feel when we do not respond correctly to conviction. Guilt is not a factual judgement about what you did or did not do. Guilt says, "You are not good," or "You are wrong." Guilt happens when you do not respond correctly to God's conviction of wrong. We feel guilty because we do not make it right.
That is, we begin to feel bad about ourselves and our actions. We begin to feel horrible, unworthy, and question whether God is mad at us. Feeling guilty is feeling shame, and it is not a feeling from God. Guilt is not of God. Guilt is what happens to us emotionally when we fail to accept that God has forgiven us. Guilt will destroy us. Guilt is a weapon against us.

Some healthy emotions accompany the conviction of wrong -- guilt is not one of them. It is okay to feel regret in the moment of conviction. We all want to please God. No one wants to mess up. But that regret should be fleeting as you respond to the Holy Spirit's conviction. After all, when we follow, we feel great about following.

When you feel guilty, it is time to seek God, accept His forgiveness, and respond to the Holy Spirit's conviction.

❽ Is there anything you feel guilty about right now? How can you fix what you are doing wrong and remove the feeling of guilt?

_____

_____

QUICK, SMART START

HOW DOES THE SPIRIT CHANGE US?

Conviction is one of our first tangible interactions with God, but the Spirit does much more in us. The Spirit changes us, renews us, and empowers us to live our new lives.

One of the most incredible things the Holy Spirit does is restore parts of us that withered away because of sin. You were designed to be complete only when you were connected, united, and filled with God's Spirit. Having his Spirit joined with your spirit was the original design (see **Genesis 2:7, John 20:22**). Now that you are a believer, the Holy Spirit is back at work in you, completing you and restoring essential parts of your being.

Interestingly, the very things the Spirit produces are the very things we all want. Paul describes these qualities as the fruits of the Spirit in Galatians 5:23-23. And he reminds us these incredible qualities are only produced by a close relationship with the Holy Spirit. The fruit of the Spirit consists of:

- Love
- Joy
- Peace
- Patience
- Kindness
- Goodness
- Faithfulness
- Gentleness
- Self-Control

How many people have prayed for patience? How many of us long for self-control? According to God, both are produced by His Spirit rather than developed by us. He produces love and faithfulness as the Holy Spirit works in our lives. The fruits of the Spirit are merely byproducts of a healthy relationship with God. We should be asking God for his Spirit or asking him to fill us with his Spirit instead of asking for patience. Patience is already inside of us. It is the Holy Spirit's gift. It is what the Holy Spirit brings to the table. God has restored us to our original design, and the Spirit provides patience.

Genesis 2:7

Then the Lord God formed the man of dust from the ground, and breathed into his nostrils the breath of life; and the man became a living person. NASB

John 20:22

And when He had said this, He breathed on them and said to them, "Receive the Holy Spirit.

So why do we continue to struggle with impatience? We are not walking in the Spirit, relying on the Spirit, and listening to the Spirit of God deep inside us. Following God's ways, talking to God, and worshipping God leads to a life where the Holy Spirit empowers us. Joy, peace, and all the spiritual fruit are gifts that God has already given us by placing his Spirit inside us.

9 Stop for a minute and write a prayer to God, asking him to unleash the fruits of His Spirit in your life. Be honest and surrender yourself to Him.

_____

_____

_____

HOW CAN I AVOID SIN?

Day 8

Christians often talk about being filled with the Spirit. The Bible contains examples and teachings about Christians being filled with the Spirit. But the Bible is clear, the Spirit is immediately inside everyone who believes. If Christians already have the Spirit of God in them, why would they ever need to be filled again?

Grudem, in his work entitled "Systematic Theology" defines being filled with the Spirit as,

> an event subsequent to conversion in which a believer experiences a fresh infilling with the Holy Spirit that may result in a variety of consequences, including greater love for God, greater victory over sin, greater power for ministry, and sometimes the receiving of new spiritual gifts

Paul tells the Ephesians to be filled with the Spirit in **Ephesians 5:18-19**. Being filled with the Spirit is like being over-taken and empowered by a fresh fire of God. And we see God fill a group of believers filled with the Spirit when they pray for help. These believers already had the Spirit. In fact, the Spirit was doing incredible works through them. But when they

Ephesians 5:18-19

Don't be drunk with wine, because that will ruin your life. Instead, be filled with the Holy Spirit, singing psalms and hymns and spiritual songs among yourselves, and making music to the Lord in your hearts.

prayed for help, Luke describes the result as them being filled with the Spirit.

> And now, Lord, look upon their threats and grant to your servants to continue to speak your word with all boldness, while you stretch out your hand to heal, and signs and wonders are performed through the name of your holy servant Jesus." And when they had prayed, the place in which they were gathered together was shaken, and they were all filled with the Holy Spirit and continued to speak the word of God with boldness.
>
> Acts 4:29-31 ESV

Being filled with the Spirit isn't about you getting more of the Spirit. Being filled with the Spirit is about the Holy Spirit getting more of you.

The filling of the Holy Spirit is not you getting more of the Holy Spirit. You were given the Holy Spirit when you got saved. The Spirit is a person. You cannot get more of him. The Biblical phrase "being filled with the Spirit" is about the Holy Spirit getting more of you. Being filled with the Spirit allows the Spirit to invade every part and moment of your life. Being filled with the Spirit is letting the power of the Spirit flow through your being. Being filled with the Spirit is God unleashing a new wave of power, inspiration, and grace in your life.

You can even ask God to fill you with the Holy Spirit.

> What father among you, if his son asks for a fish, will instead of a fish give him a serpent; or if he asks for an egg, will give him a scorpion? If you then, who are evil, know how to give good gifts to your children, how much more will the heavenly Father give the Holy Spirit to those who ask him!"
>
> Luke 11:11-13 ESV

You can ask God to take you over. You can ask God for increasing presence in every area of your life. You are setting yourself aside and making room for your miraculous God to work in you. You ask him to produce spiritual fruit and guide your every moment, feeling, and perception. People filled with the Spirit always have an attitude of joy toward God. Letting the Word of Christ richly dwell in you results in this same attitude.

> Let the message about Christ, in all its richness, fill your lives. Teach and counsel each other with all the wisdom he gives. Sing psalms and hymns and spiritual songs to God with thankful hearts. 17And whatever you do or say, do it as a representative of the Lord Jesus, giving thanks through him to God the Father.
>
> Colossians 3:16-17 NLT

A person who saturates his mind with the Word of God is ready for the Spirit of God to bring his truths to life. Galatians 5:16-17 reminds us to let the Spirit take over and reform our desires.

> So I say, let the Holy Spirit guide your lives. Then you won't be doing what your sinful nature craves. The sinful nature wants to do evil, which is just the opposite of what the Spirit wants. And the Spirit gives us desires that are the opposite of what the sinful nature desires. These two forces are constantly fighting each other, so you are not free to carry out your good intentions.
>
> Galatians 5:16-17 NLT

You can do this by simply walking in the Spirit. Walking in the Spirit is listening to God's words and voice in real-time. Walking in the Spirit is seeking God. Walking in the Spirit has powerful results.

Do you feel dry? Are you tired? Do you want the fruit of the Spirit to grow in your life? Do you need deliverance? Ask God to "fill you" as you abandon yourself to His life, His will, His desires, His words, His instructions, and His love. Allow the Holy Spirit to control your life.

 Take a minute and write your memory verse in the margin.

AT THE END OF THE WEEK ANSWER THESE QUESTIONS

What was the most meaningful statement(s) or scripture this week?	Reword the statement or scripture into a prayer of response to God.	What actions do you need to take in response to this week's study?
_____	_____	_____
_____	_____	_____
_____	_____	_____
_____	_____	_____
_____	_____	_____

TRUTH 6

MEMORY VERSE

Devote yourselves to prayer with an alert mind and a thankful heart.

Colossians 4:2

Prayer

What Women Want

Several years ago, I taught our congregation a message titled "What Women Want." I am not sure what I was thinking. The ladies loved it, the men had to listen, and the single crowd was the single crowd. But as I prepared, I learned a few things.

I wanted to teach the Bible, so I looked at all those classic verses about what godly men should look like and do. I also sent out a survey to all the women in our church asking, "What do you wish men would know about women? What is the one thing you would tell them?" I was amazed at the response (every lady responded), but I was more surprised at the answers.

There were brutally honest thoughts about intimacy and not rushing romance. Things like, "This is a partnership" and "I am not your maid." There were insightful thoughts about husbands and boyfriends acting like men instead of children. There were requests like, "Tell the men that ladies love knights in shining armor." But head and shoulders above all the answers was one simple idea, "I want him to listen, really listen to me."

The ladies said it in different ways, but they wanted their husbands to listen and engage in quality conversation. As I displayed the answers on the big screen (anonymously, of course), I shuddered when my wife's response received a standing ovation. Her answer was, "I want him to listen to the end."

So often, we don't really listen. Our brains are busy, and, quite frankly, we are selfish. We want to be listened to or do our own thing. God reminded me that day that he wants to talk to me and with me. And, I need to pay attention and listen to the end.

QUICK, SMART START

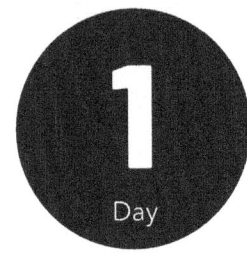

WHAT IS PRAYER?

"How do I pray?" is one of the most common questions Christians ask. It seems like we are insecure when it comes to talking with God. We believe we need to please him, an idea that God only responds to certain types of prayer. If you have ever wondered if you are praying correctly, you are not alone. In fact, if you have ever asked around or done a web search, you know there are as many answers to that question as there are opinions. Some emphasize praying for others (the fancy name is intercessory prayer.) Some emphasize praying for your needs. Some emphasize thanking God for everything before you ask for things. Others tell you to pray in the Spirit, leaving you wondering, "What is that?"

There are prayer conferences, prayer methods, and model prayers. Everyone seems to be trying to figure out how to pray. It makes sense, though. After all, our faith began with a prayer. A prayer that someone led us in. They told us how to pray for salvation. There is no doubt that prayer is essential.

Prayer is just a spiritual word for having a conversation with God.

❶ Take a minute to review your memory verse for this week. Write it below.

_____

_____

We need to talk to God and hear from God to have a relationship with him. You see it in the great followers before Jesus came and after Jesus left. You see it as Jesus as he went off to be alone and hear from God.

The problem is not with our desire to communicate effectively with God. The problem is that we are asking the wrong question. What most of us need to ask is, "What is prayer?"

When the disciples asked Jesus to teach them how to pray, Jesus taught them big concepts. If you search the Bible looking for "How do I pray?" you will find only one answer, which was given to a specific group, in a specific moment, for a specific purpose. The Bible does not answer the question, "How do I pray?" It does not provide systems and methods.

However, if you search the Bible looking for "What is prayer?" you will find hundreds of examples of people praying to God. You will see their success and their empty prayers. You will see God answering them and not answering them. And you will find the answer to "What is prayer?".

Prayer is just a spiritual word for having a conversation with God. Every example of prayer is people having a conversation with God. Asking, "How do I pray?" is like asking, "How do I talk to God?". The answer, of course, is just to talk. The people who prayed in the Bible were talking to God. Sometimes they started a conversation. Sometimes God started the conversation. Sometimes they asked for wisdom. Sometimes they told God how much they loved him. Sometimes they recalled all his great works. Sometimes they asked for help. Sometimes they "dumped on" God. Prayer is just a two-way conversation with God. If you can talk, you can pray. He loves you, and he loves listening. He is your heavenly Father, and he loves talking, sharing, and guiding. You can start to talk, or he can begin to speak. You can speak aloud or quietly in your heart and mind. You never know; he might even speak audibly to you one day. No matter, prayer is just a spiritual word for talking with God.

Colossians 4:2

Devote yourselves to prayer with an alert mind and a thankful heart.

❷ Has God started a conversation with you? Try this exercise. Write down the last time you felt the question deep inside you, "Should you be doing this?"

_____

_____

_____

Feeling conviction is God beginning a conversation with you. He is convicting you. He is speaking to you. But God also starts other conversations. Perhaps, while reading the Bible, the Spirit, God, inspires you to see a new, fresh truth. It is as if God is saying, "Look at that!" Have you been talking to someone and knew God wanted you to encourage that person? That is God beginning a conversation. Your next step is to ask, "What do you want me to say?"

Prayer can be as puzzling as understanding the Holy Spirit. But your relationship with God is like every other relationship. Relationships need communication to stay healthy. We need God. We need Him to guide us, to teach us the Bible, and to help us make the right decisions. And, He wants to talk to us. Your personal relationship with Jesus Christ cannot grow without proper communication. So relax and just talk to him.

QUICK, SMART START

WHAT IS THE PURPOSE OF PRAYER?

Does a conversation have to have a specific purpose? What is the purpose of talking to a friend? There may be many purposes or no purpose whatsoever. We talk because we want and need to communicate with others. Why do you talk to your friends? Sometimes you need to know something. Sometimes you want to hear about their day. Sometimes they start a conversation. Sometimes you simply listen.

Spending time talking and listening to God is no different. Prayer brings peace to our lives as we share our problems, concerns, and needs with Him. We learn as we listen to the Spirit of God inside of us. We hear conviction. We can ask for direction ahead of time. We can talk to God about anything.

> Don't worry about anything, but in everything, through prayer and petition with thanksgiving, let your requests be made known to God. And the peace of God, which surpasses every thought, will guard your hearts and your minds in Christ Jesus.
>
> Philippians 4:6-7 HCSB

Matthew 6:8 HCSB

...your Father knows the things you need before you ask Him.

God is aware of your needs and challenges. He wants to help, and he wants to bring peace to your mind. When we pray, the Holy Spirit can grow the fruit of peace in our lives. You need to feel comfortable crying out to God and asking for help. God says,

> Call on Me in a day of trouble; I will rescue you, and you will honor Me.
>
> Psalm 50:15 HCSB

You draw close to God by listening as much as you speak. In this intimate relationship, God can prove his sufficiency for every need. He is active in every detail of your life and knows exactly what you need even before you ask (see **Matthew 6:8**).

Imagine listening to God and hearing, "Your boss will try to cheat you. You need to find a new job. Call that new warehouse down the road." It sounds crazy, but the more you read the Bible, the more you will see that

God speaks to those who take the time to listen. He tells us things we could never know and answers questions we would never know to ask.

❸ Has there ever been a time when you were certain (convicted, convinced by God deep down inside) of something going on or coming soon that you could never have known on your own? If so, describe it below. If not, write a quick prayer to God and ask him to develop this type of relationship in you.

_____

_____

_____

_____

> **1 Kings 4:29-34**
>
> God gave Solomon very great wisdom and understanding…he could speak with authority about all kinds of plants…he could also speak about animals, birds, small creatures, and fish. And kings from every nation sent their ambassadors to listen to the wisdom of Solomon.

Try asking God to read your Bible with you. Asking the unseen God to sit down and read with you is mystical, but think how practical it is. God said the Holy Spirit would be your teacher. You are asking him to do the very thing he promised to do. Now that is a prayer that God will certainly answer! God longs to give wisdom and to guide anyone who will give him the time and listen.

Prayer is also a great asset in decision-making. Start that conversation by asking, "God is this really the best dishwasher? Can you help me find information?" He said, "Ask anything" — we should. Solomon was the wisest man who ever lived. He asked God to make him wise, and God went over the top. God gave him spiritual wisdom and made him incredibly smart in science, art, math, and biology too. People traveled from afar to learn from Solomon (see **1 Kings 4:29-34**). Involving God in big decisions and work decisions is the essence of walking and talking with God. This is what Paul meant when he said,

> Never stop praying.
>
> 1 Thessalonians 5:17

You do not have to live in a cave or have a special closet to dedicate yourself to prayer. Dedicated prayer is being available to talk with God whenever He wishes. Faithful prayer involves starting all those crazy conversations like thanking him for your dog. Prayer does not have to have a specific purpose. But purposefully taking the time to sit, talk, and listen to God is the pathway to a great relationship.

QUICK, SMART START

④ Take a few minutes to simply talk to God. Write down anything he talks to you about. It may feel odd, but stop and say, "Hi." Then just have a conversation.

_____

_____

_____

_____

HOW DO I PRAY?

First, talk to God as your friend. He is your friend!

> You are My friends if you do what I command you. I do not call you slaves anymore, because a slave doesn't know what his master is doing. I have called you friends, because I have made known to you everything I have heard from My Father.
>
> John 15:14-15 HCSB

Second, pray always – develop a lifestyle of talking to God like you would that new love of your life.

> Devote yourselves to prayer with an alert mind and a thankful heart.
>
> Colossians 4:2 NLT

Third, pray about everything. Talk to God about how you feel. Talk to him as you think through problems. Listen to him and for him continuously.

> Rejoice always, pray without ceasing, give thanks in all circumstances; for this is the will of God in Christ Jesus for you.
>
> 1 Thessalonians 5:17-18 ESV

God desires that you talk with him all the time. He wants to hear from you. He wants to guide you. And He wants to spend time with you. You do not have to convince God, beg God, or try to impress Him with many words. You do not need to repeat words to create focus. In fact, Jesus warned about this religious, impressing God type of prayer.

> When you pray, don't babble like the idolaters, since they imagine they'll be heard for their many words.
>
> Matthew 6:7 HCSB

So talk to God in your own language as if speaking to a friend.

> Inside the Tent of Meeting, the Lord would speak to Moses face to face, as one speaks to a friend. Afterward, Moses would return to the camp, but the young man who assisted him, Joshua son of Nun, would remain behind in the Tent of Meeting.
>
> Exodus 33:11 NLT

❺ Have you ever heard a "cheesy" sounding prayer or a prayer that seemed more about the person praying than the prayer itself? What bothered you about that prayer? Write your answer below.

_____

_____

_____

_____

Did you notice Joshua in the verse above? Joshua was an ordinary assistant, but he stood in the presence of God and heard God speak. You have direct access to God and do not need to go through any other person to talk to Him. How incredibly encouraging is that?

> For there is one God and one mediator between God and man, a man, Christ Jesus, who gave Himself—a ransom for all, a testimony at the proper time.
>
> 1 Timothy 2:5-6 HCSB

Jesus paved the way for you to speak with the Father as his child. To talk to Jesus as his friend. And you have the Holy Spirit, your broadband connection to God.

> For through Him (Jesus) we both have access by one Spirit to the Father.
>
> Ephesians 2:18 HCSB

You are connected to God because you are in a relationship with God. He started that relationship, and he wants it to continue. Tell God when you are thankful. Let Him know how much you love him. Pray for others. Share with Him all those things that are on your heart and mind. Just talk to Him.

ARE THERE THINGS THAT CAN MESS UP MY PRAYER LIFE?

God always hears our prayers, but he may not speak. Some things can interrupt your conversation with God. For example, unconfessed sin will definitely hinder your prayer life. It can prevent you from feeling confident as you talk to God.

Your relationship with God is a real relationship. How interrupted are your friendships when friends do you wrong and do not make it right? How difficult is it to invest in your child until he admits his error and is ready to correct his behavior? Your friend is still your friend. Your child is always your child. But, there is not much to talk about until they make it right. Your relationship with God is no different.

Confessing and owning our offenses against our Father allows us to restore good communication. This is why John encourages us, saying,

> But if we are living in the light, as God is in the light, then we have fellowship with each other, and the blood of Jesus, his Son, cleanses us from all sin. If we claim we have no sin, we are only fooling ourselves and not living in the truth. But if we confess our sins to him, he is faithful and just to forgive us our sins and to cleanse us from all wickedness.
>
> 1 John 1:7-9 NLT

Are there any unconfessed sins in your life right now? Are there things you have not resolved with God or talked to him about? Write your answer below, and take a minute to admit your sin and ask for forgiveness.

_____

_____

Another thing that can get in the way of talking to and hearing answers from God — not believing. James taught about this exact thing. He encourages us with these words,

> If any of you lacks wisdom, let him ask God, who gives generously to all without reproach, and it will be given him.
>
> James 1:5 ESV

In other words, ask God, and he will answer. God loves talking and responding. You do not have to wander around wondering. Just ask. But James added another important truth. You should not expect to hear anything if you are not going to act on God's answers.

> But let him ask in faith, with no doubting, for the one who doubts is like a wave of the sea that is driven and tossed by the wind. For that person must not suppose that he will receive anything from the Lord; he is a double-minded man, unstable in all his ways.
>
> James 1:6-8 ESV

If you want answers, you must believe God will answer and be committed to following His direction. It makes sense. How often will you answer your friend who never takes your advice?

Another thing that can interrupt your prayers is not doing what you already know. The Bible is full of truths, commands, principles, and answers. God expects that we will read his Word and remember his Word (see **Deuteronomy 6:1-3**). In fact, one of the jobs of the Holy Spirit is reminding you of the truths you have already read. But, if you ignore what he has taught you, if you do not adjust your life to his truths, it will hinder your prayer life. This is how God put it.

> God detests the prayers of a person who ignores the law.
>
> Proverbs 28:9 NLT

The laws were God's instructions to the people of Israel. Solomon teaches us that God is not prone to speak with those who are ignoring his

Deuteronomy 6:1-3

These are the commands, decrees, and regulations that the Lord your God commanded me to teach you. You must obey them in the land you are about to enter and occupy, and you and your children and grandchildren must fear the Lord your God as long as you live. If you obey all his decrees and commands, you will enjoy a long life. Listen closely, Israel, and be careful to obey. Then all will go well with you, and you will have many children in the land flowing with milk and honey, just as the Lord, the God of your ancestors, promised you.

directions for living. Disobedient living hinders the Spirit in us and messes up our prayer life because the Spirit is God. He is our link to God.

But, the most obvious thing that prevents us from hearing from God is that we do not ask or ask with hidden motives. When it comes to asking for things, James taught the followers of God,

> You do not have because you do not ask. You ask and don't receive because you ask wrongly, so that you may spend it on your desires for pleasure.
>
> James 4:2 HCSB

If we do not ask, then we may never receive. You need to ask God for what you need.

❼ Reflect on your current situations in life. Is there anything that you have not asked God about? Is there anything you are trying to handle on your own? If so, take a moment and write a prayer to him.

_____

_____

_____

_____

If we do not ask, then we may never receive. You need to ask God for what you need. But, if you ask for your selfish desires, God may not answer. God is a loving Father. He does not want to give you something that he knows is not good for you to have. Like a loving parent, he is not going to reward selfishness.

There are also prayers that God cannot answer. There are things he cannot give us. Praying that God will save your brother is an example. God will not force your brother to be saved because God has given your brother free choice. However, you could pray that God would soften your brother's heart or show Himself to your brother. You could ask God to change your brother's circumstances so that he seeks God. Pray for things that are consistent with what you know about God.

Follow God well, read the Bible, do not hinder the Spirit, believe in His answers, be committed to following, and you will hear from God.

Are there any quick tips on prayers?

There is much to learn about prayer, and you will grow in your ability to hear God's voice. Start by keeping it simple. Do you believe you can hear the voice of God? How do you know when it is God speaking versus you just thinking? Remember, prayer is a conversation.

Let me take you back to the last time you were tempted. How did you know you were tempted? Did you hear a loving voice in your heart saying, "No!"? That was God. You have the Spirit of God inside you, and his Spirit speaks to your spirit. The same voice that says "No" can say "Yes." That same "No" voice can say, "Hey Bob, maybe you should look at that stock deal," or "Mary, something is up with your daughter." We are so familiar with the voice we hear in conviction. That is likely the same voice he will use in all our other conversations.

❽ What does it feel like when God convicts you? How do you hear him? Have you heard that voice in another situation? Write your answers below.

_____

_____

_____

Listen for God like you did when you waited for those phone calls from your first love. Look for God like you check your texts for your best friend's response.

Here are a few quick tips on prayer:

- Always talk to God about everything, anytime, all the time. Why wouldn't you? As I sat down to write these words, I asked God to write through me. When making decisions, I listen to people. Still, simultaneously I am asking God to remind me of his truths and give me real-time direction.

- Set aside a specific time to talk to God. Make an appointment with Him every day to talk to him about your day. Tell God what was great about the day. Tell him what was not so great. See what He has to say. Making an appointment is an excellent habit for life, and it helps as you start your relationship with God. We tend to forget God because we cannot see him in the kitchen. We tend to

> **Philippians 4:6**
>
> Don't worry about anything; instead, pray about everything. Tell God what you need, and thank him for all he has done.

> **Romans 8:26**
>
> And the Holy Spirit helps us in our weakness. For example, we don't know what God wants us to pray for. But the Holy Spirit prays for us with groanings that cannot be expressed in words.

miss the fact that he may have things to say. Make a daily appointment just to talk.

- You know what you need or want, so ask. James taught us that we do not have because we do not ask. Paul taught the Philippians to tell God their requests (see **Philippians 4:6**). Never be afraid to ask God for exactly what you want. Do not beat around the bush or try to impress God with a bunch of thank-yous. He knows your heart. Just ask and ask specifically.

- Use a journal and keep track of your conversations. Keep track of your trials, aha moments, and requests. Remembering what we prayed and how God answered those prayers is fun. Keeping track of what we pray helps us to see God at work in and around us.

- Do not worry when you run out of words. Sometimes we hurt, we long, or we need to sit with our best friends. Sometimes we are quiet. You can be the same with God. If you are overwhelmed, be comfortably quiet; know that the Holy Spirit is always praying for you even when you do not know how to pray (see **Romans 8:26**).

- Take whatever answer you get. God will talk to us. He loves talking to us. But, he may not always answer your prayers the way or in the timeframe you want. God is your Heavenly Father. All His ways are perfect. Sometimes, the best answer to your prayer will be "NO" or "NOT YET." Other times he might make you aware that you need to correct something in your life. In all those times, take whatever answer you get.

- Pray for others. Paul prayed for others continually (see Romans 1:9) and requested prayer on many occasions (see Hebrews 13:18; 2 Thessalonians 3:1). Lift people up and pray for them.

❾ Take a minute and write out your memory verse.

_____

_____

_____

10 In your own words, what is the purpose of this lesson?

_____

_____

_____

AT THE END OF THE WEEK ANSWER THESE QUESTIONS

What was the most meaningful statement(s) or scripture this week?	Reword the statement or scripture into a prayer of response to God.	What actions do you need to take in response to this week's study?
_____	_____	_____
_____	_____	_____
_____	_____	_____
_____	_____	_____
_____	_____	_____
_____	_____	_____

TRUTH 7

MEMORY VERSE

Therefore, brothers, by the mercies of God, I urge you to present your bodies as a living sacrifice, holy and pleasing to God; this is your spiritual worship. Do not be conformed to this age, but be transformed by the renewing of your mind, so that you may discern what is the good, pleasing, and perfect will of God.

Romans 12:1-2

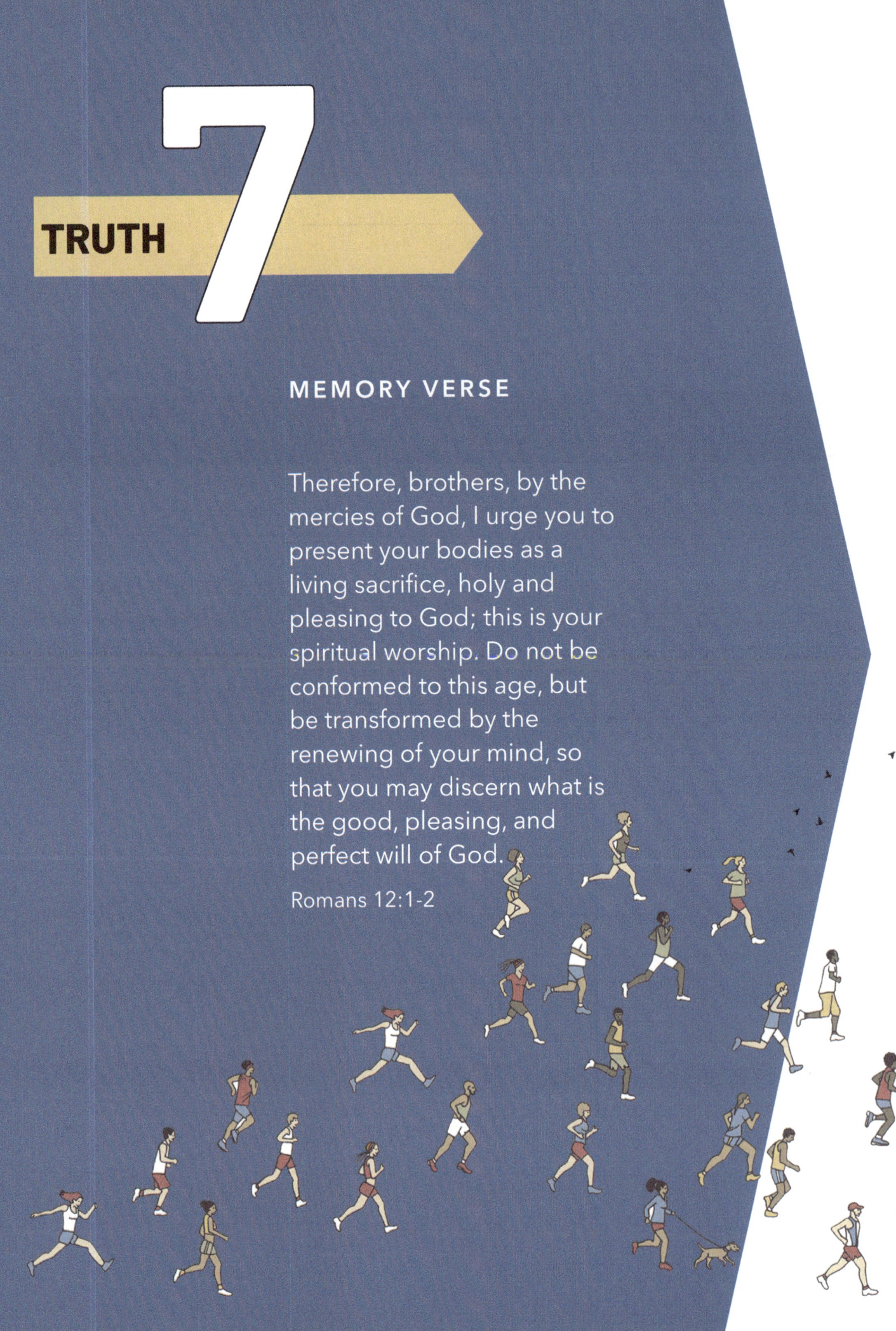

The Will of God

My Smart Friend Alan

Our church has been seeing God work in the area of making disciples. It started when we got serious about trying to help people follow Christ and mature. Ten years later, we have nine generations of healthy disciples making disciples themselves. It is like a dream come true!

The movement has now grown beyond us. My time has become increasingly taxed with travel, meetings, writing, and speaking as other churches ask us to show them what God showed us. Balancing God's call to lead our church, teach, and help other churches has created a crisis of belief for me. How will all this get done? How long can I sustain this pace? Does God really want me to champion others in disciple making? Does he want me to step back at church?

I have a friend who is at the same point in his world. Alan is one of the most generous, caring, incredible worship leaders on the planet earth. He not only leads worship teams, he disciples worship leaders. Over the past year, Alan has been feeling an ambiguous call to do more. He has taken short sabbaticals, talked with his pastor, and asked for prayer. I know his frustration at figuring out the next step.

We were chatting over text, and Alan said this incredible thing. "You know Doug, I have been challenged to focus less on what is coming and focus more on doing what I know God has right in front of me." Wow! What a great reminder. A couple of years ago, when the stress of going public and helping others get started, God said something similar in my heart. "Just do what I put in front of you. Don't worry about anyone or anything else," I heard him say. I felt such great peace. Funny how I seem to have forgotten that truth. How great that God reminded me through a friend.

You don't have to figure it all out. God will guide you along the way.

WHAT DOES GOD WANT ME TO DO?

"What does God want you to do?" It is a good question. It makes sense. You have abandoned yourself to follow this incredible Savior and God. Now, you want to know how to live this life. You want to know the best thing to do in every situation. You want to serve God. You realize your ways can be flawed. You simply want to know what God desires and follow him. You want to get it right for Him, your family, and your employees.

Sometimes, we can be a bit performance-oriented, not wanting to tick God off. We do not want to fail. Other times, we have a healthier attitude. We want to succeed. We want to please God. We want to get this right. Whether we are working on future plans or just trying to make a decision today, it is only natural to desire God's input. You have recognized that his ways are better and want to know how to live this life. That is great! You want to know what you do not know. You do not want to miss out on something great God has for you.

You hear verses like,

> For I know the plans I have for you," says the Lord. "They are plans for good and not for disaster, to give you a future and a hope.
>
> Jeremiah 29:11

and you realize that God may actually have a plan. Many Christians refer to this "big direction" for our lives as the will of God. And Christians are continually talking about finding His will for their lives. But the will of God can be a confusing topic. Here are a few examples:

- Doing-oriented believers are looking for the next new thing to do with God, for God, and in their lives.
- Relationship-oriented believers claim that God's will is for us to live a personal Christian life and follow God moment by moment.
- Bigger picture believers ask God, "Where do I fit in your plan to help people and save the world?"
- Less confident believers ask for things adding "if it is your will" at the end of their prayers.

THE WILL OF GOD

In a way, all these believers are all right, and it can still leave us wondering if we can actually know what God wants us to do. We have the Holy Spirit of God in our lives. We know God can speak to us. He can convince us to do this or that. There are times we are confident God wants us to do something specific. But, other times, it seems we cannot hear him. Worse yet, all the answers we need are not in the Bible.

Does God care what car you buy? What college should I attend? Should I get serious with this guy? Should I take that job? Should I go on that mission trip? The Bible does not answer these questions. What does God want? We hear people say that God wants them to do something, and then we see them change their minds again and again. If God wants them to do something, why would he change his mind later?

The whole thing can get really frustrating, and, sadly, many followers just give up. But, there is hope. The will of God is actually pretty easy to find in the Bible. There are answers to some specific decisions. You can find principles to guide you in those areas the Bible does not explicitly address. You can know what God's will is. You can discover his plan for you. You can know what He wants you to do.

You can know what God's will is. You can discover his plan for you. You can know what He wants you to do.

❶ Circle the type of believer you are from the list on the previous page. If you feel like more than one type, circle as many as apply.

❷ Take a minute to review your memory verse for this week. Write it below.

_____

_____

_____

_____

_____

QUICK, SMART START

WHAT IS THE WILL OF GOD?

Christians often confuse God's will with God's plan for their lives. God may have definite plans for your life, but His will is never connected with a set of rules, a geographical location, a particular person, or a specific thing to do. God's will is much more conceptual. God's will is like a bigger picture. It is spiritual, not physical.

God's will is about what he desires for creation, for the world, and for humankind. God's will is about the grand scheme of things. The Bible reveals God's will again and again.

❸ Underline what you think the will of God is in each of the following verses.

> I urge you, first of all, to pray for all people. Ask God to help them; intercede on their behalf, and give thanks for them. Pray this way for kings and all who are in authority so that we can live peaceful and quiet lives marked by godliness and dignity. This is good and pleases God our Savior, who wants everyone to be saved and to understand the truth.
>
> 1 Timothy 2:1-4 NLT

> Rejoice always, pray without ceasing, give thanks in all circumstances; for this is the will of God in Christ Jesus for you.
>
> 1 Thessalonians 5:16-18 ESV

> For the Lord's sake, submit to all human authority—whether the king as head of state, or the officials he has appointed. For the king has sent them to punish those who do wrong and to honor those who do right. It is God's will that your honorable lives should silence those ignorant people who make foolish accusations against you.
>
> 1 Peter 2:13-15 NLT

> For this is God's will, your sanctification: that you abstain from sexual immorality so that each of you knows how to possess his own vessel in sanctification and honor, not with lustful desires, like the Gentiles who don't know God. This means one must not transgress against and defraud his brother in this matter, because the Lord is an avenger of all these offenses, as we also previously told and warned you. For God has not called us to impurity, but to sanctification. Therefore, the person who rejects this does not reject man, but God, who also gives you His Holy Spirit.
>
> 1 Thessalonians 4:3-8 HCSB

God's will is that everyone be saved. His will is that we be thankful and peacemakers (reflecting the character of God.) It is God's will that we live honorable lives — our new lives. God's will is that each of us allows the Holy Spirit to sanctify us (cleanse us of the old and transform our minds and actions to reflect our new life in Christ.)

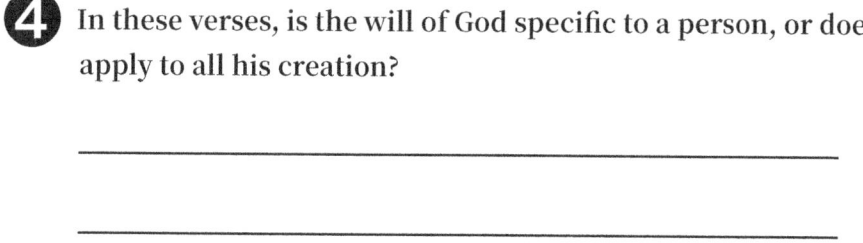 **In these verses, is the will of God specific to a person, or does it apply to all his creation?**

_____

_____

The will of God is the same for every person on earth. The plans of God are more specific to times, people groups, situations, and individuals. Here is another description of the will of God.

> We know that all things work together for the good of those who love God: those who are called according to His purpose. For those He foreknew He also predestined to be conformed to the image of His Son, so that He would be the firstborn among many brothers.
>
> Romans 8:28-29 HCSB

It is God's will (his desire) that everyone gets saved, and it is His will (something he will accomplish) that all the saved be conformed to the image of His Son. Not everyone will be saved. Not everyone will choose to believe in Him. Not everyone will follow Him. But you have a relationship with God (you are saved), and in that, you have fulfilled the will of God. If you walk with God allowing him to transform you, you are fulfilling His will.

God's will is:

- That everyone has a restored relationship with Him -- be saved.
- That we are thankful in everything for God.
- That we are doing well and living pure personal lives.

The will of God is the big picture of God's desires for his creation. It is not a specific plan for anyone's life. Instead, his will is the foundation of those plans. Perhaps the best summary of God's will for you is found in Luke 10:27.

> You shall love the Lord your God with all your heart, and with all your soul, and with all your strength, and with all your mind; and your neighbor as yourself.
>
> Luke 10:27 NASB

Jesus, the Son of God, came to earth to show us God's love. He invites us to love God and return to him. God's will (that everyone is saved and conformed to his image) was Jesus' entire reason for coming to earth. He put it this way,

> I came that they may have life and have it abundantly. I am the good shepherd. The good shepherd lays down his life for the sheep.
>
> John 10:10-11 ESV

HOW DO I FIND GOD'S PLAN FOR MY LIFE?

It is good to want to discover God's plan for your life. It is wise to ask God if he has a long-range plan for you. But, God is far more interested in you being the type of person He wants you to be than you doing mighty works. The most natural way to discover God's plan for your life is to follow Him in each moment. The very simple secret to discovering God's plan for you is,

> Be who He wants you to be, and He will show you what to do along the way.

Jesus put it this way,

> Those who accept my commandments and obey them are the ones who love me. And because they love me, my Father will love them. And I will love them and reveal myself to each of them.
> John 14:21

People who are in a relationship read each other's love letters. They talk to each other. They learn from one another. They move through life together. It is the same with God. We are in a relationship with God when we read his words (the Bible), talk with him (pray), and listen to His Spirit guiding us. He speaks to those that are listening. He speaks to those that are applying everything they already know about God. You will find God's advice, his direction, and his plans for you as you have a relationship with Him.

Paul put it this way,

> Therefore, brothers, by the mercies of God, I urge you to present your bodies as a living sacrifice, holy and pleasing to God; this is your spiritual worship. Do not be conformed to this age, but be transformed by the renewing of your mind, so that you may discern what is the good, pleasing, and perfect will of God.
> Romans 12:1-2 HCSB

Paul teaches that we will discover God's will for humankind if we follow God. He also says we will find the "plans of God" for us in that same relationship. Again we hear,

> Be who He wants you to be, and He will show you what to do along the way.

God's will and plan are found as you have a relationship with God, renew your mind, and follow his ways. Preparing yourself to do whatever He wants broadens the opportunities for God to use you. Being exposed to God's truths provides fuel for decisions and life plans. The Bible is full of principles and specific answers to guide our choices and direction.

Part of your specific plan will always be being a part of God's bigger plan. Paul tells us to renew our minds to have the same attitude that Christ had.

> *You will find God's advice, his direction, and his plans for you as you have a relationship with Him.*

QUICK, SMART START

> Don't look out only for your own interests, but take an interest in others, too. You must have the same attitude that Christ Jesus had. Though he was God, he did not think of equality with God as something to cling to. Instead, he gave up his divine privileges; he took the humble position of a slave and was born as a human being. When he appeared in human form, he humbled himself in obedience to God and died a criminal's death on a cross.
>
> Philippians 2:4-8

Be who He wants you to be, and He will show you what to do along the way.

Jesus put the salvation of the world above everything else. He became a living part of the plan to reconcile the whole world to God. Part of your specific plan is being a part of that same plan. Whether you are trying to find answers, advice, or direction, your goal should be to align your worldly thoughts with the thoughts of God. As you follow God and apply his truths, you can trust Him to guide you in the detailed plan, step by step.

❺ How is your relationship with God? Are you in love? Are you passionate? Is God revealing himself and his ways to you?

_____

_____

_____

❻ How are you involved in God's plan to save everyone?

_____

_____

_____

_____

HOW DO I TALK WITH GOD ABOUT MY PLANS AND HIS PLANS?

You are not alone if you struggle to figure out how to talk with God about your plans and His plans. The disciples walked with Jesus every day. They had immediate access to all God's wisdom, but even they asked, "Lord, teach us to pray." So Jesus taught them, and he used an interesting story along the way.

> Then, teaching them more about prayer, he used this story: "Suppose you went to a friend's house at midnight, wanting to borrow three loaves of bread. You say to him, 'A friend of mine has just arrived for a visit, and I have nothing for him to eat.' And suppose he calls out from his bedroom, 'Don't bother me. The door is locked for the night, and my family and I are all in bed. I can't help you.' But I tell you this—though he won't do it for friendship's sake, if you keep knocking long enough, he will get up and give you whatever you need because of your shameless persistence.
>
> Luke 11:5-8

You can imagine them wondering what this had to do with prayer. But, Jesus explained it.

> "And so I tell you, keep on asking, and you will receive what you ask for. Keep on seeking, and you will find. Keep on knocking, and the door will be opened to you. For everyone who asks, receives. Everyone who seeks, finds. And to everyone who knocks, the door will be opened.
>
> Luke 11:9-10

Jesus promised that if you keep asking, if you are persistent, God will answer. God will respond. What an incredible promise! If you need advice, if you need answers, keep asking. If you need help with a decision if you want to involve God in planning your future life, keep asking. He promises to answer. He promises to be found by and help the persistent disciple. The Holy Spirit can convince you that a particular direction is correct. The Spirit can show you an answer in the Bible. He might remind you of a principle that you have already learned. God will always answer and act on behalf of those who seek Him.

7 How confident are you in talking to God about your plans? Do you talk to him about business deals and leadership decisions? Do you talk to him before you discipline your children?

_____

_____

_____

_____

Do you remember how people think about God's will when trying to find his plan for their lives?

- Doing-oriented believers are looking for the next new thing to do with God, for God, and in their lives.
- Relationship-oriented believers claim that God's will is for us to live a personal Christian life and follow God moment by moment.
- Bigger picture believers ask God, "Where do I fit in your plan to help people and save the world?"
- Less confident believers ask for things adding "if it is your will" at the end of their prayers.

Each of these types of believers discovered part of the way to talk with God about his plan for their lives. When you are planning your future, it is good to include God. Talking with God about your next "new thing" is wise. Make an appointment with God to plan your budget. Pray with your family about your desire to relocate. Include God, asking him to remind you and show you any of his principles that can guide you. Be blunt and ask, "God is there something that you know that would be great for me to do next?"

Learn from relationship-oriented believers: being comes before doing. Live out your relationship, learn more about God, and talk with him throughout the day. Listen to the Spirit throughout the day for real-time guidance.

Embrace something bigger than your specific plan. God's plan is so much bigger than guiding your daily decisions. Figure out where you fit in God's big plan. Where is God working, and how can you get involved? How can you help others find God?

It is okay to admit that you have no clue when talking to God about your plans and his plans. It is okay to pray, "I really feel like it is time for a new job. There is this opportunity, but I don't know whether I should take it." It is okay to ask God to help you get that promotion at work. It is also okay to tag your prayer with "if it is your will." You are being honest (and God already knows your heart!) Perhaps a promotion is not in your best interest. Maybe there is something that your all-knowing God knows that you do not know. Matthew recorded an incident just like this. He wrote,

> Large crowds followed Jesus as he came down the mountainside. Suddenly, a man with leprosy approached him and knelt before him. "Lord," the man said, "if you are willing, you can heal me and make me clean." Jesus reached out and touched him. "I am willing," he said. "Be healed!" And instantly, the leprosy disappeared.
>
> Matthew 8:1-3

It is okay to admit that you have no clue when talking to God about your plans and his plans.

The leper did not know if Jesus wanted to heal him, so he added, "if you are willing." Jesus was willing to heal him, but there were other times Jesus did not heal people. Paul encountered this. God did not heal Paul when Paul asked for healing. Looking back, Paul shared this in a letter to the believers in Corinth:

> So to keep me from becoming proud, I was given a thorn in my flesh, a messenger from Satan to torment me and keep me from becoming proud. Three different times I begged the Lord to take it away. Each time he said, "My grace is all you need. My power works best in weakness."
>
> 2 Corinthians 12:7-9

Look at the honesty of his prayers. He begged God to heal him, but God did not. God only answered, "My grace is all you need." Over time, Paul realized that God allowed this difficulty to keep him humble during all his success. The plan of God can be far beyond our understanding at the moment, but we can still talk to him. It is okay to admit that you are not sure if what you are asking for is the best for you. Remember this wise proverb,

> Many are the plans in the mind of a man, but it is the purpose of the Lord that will stand.
>
> Proverbs 19:21 ESV

You need to be comfortable talking with God about all your plans:

- The plans for your future.
- The plans for your present.
- The plan for that next big decision.
- Your desire to be part of his much bigger plan.

Listen for answers while you read the Bible. Listen to the Spirit deep inside you. Talk with God like you would talk with a friend or a wise counselor.

You also need to be comfortable not knowing everything. It is unlikely that God will reveal His entire plan for your life (it would overwhelm you!) Most of us cannot conceive the incredible things that God can do in and around us as we walk with Him. Our understanding is limited. We do not see what God sees or know what he knows. We need to allow God's plans to unfold as we follow one step at a time. Be patient and wait on God while you do what you know he wants you to do right now.

❽ Have you asked God for something he did not give you? Has he shown you yet why he did not answer your request?

_____

_____

_____

❾ Take a minute and write out your memory verse.

_____

_____

_____

10 In your own words, what is the purpose of this lesson?

_____

_____

_____

AT THE END OF THE WEEK ANSWER THESE QUESTIONS

What was the most meaningful statement(s) or scripture this week?	Reword the statement or scripture into a prayer of response to God.	What actions do you need to take in response to this week's study?

It can seem confusing when you notice that Bible translators sometimes use the phrase "will of God" interchangeably. There are times when someone in the Bible says, "If you will," or "if it is your will" when what they actually mean is "I know you can do it" or "I only want you to do this if it is what is best, what you desire." Other times we read that we can "know the will of God" and the writer is referring to something bigger and more conceptual. He is actually saying, "we can know God's overall desires." The plan of God for your present situation or your future is always a part of this bigger picture - his will for all people and all of creation.

Sometimes, it seems like we are still looking for the Holy Grail when we already have it. You have a relationship with God - that was his ultimate plan, that is his ultimate will.

TRUTH 8

MEMORY VERSE

I will build my church, and all the powers of hell will not conquer it.

Matthew 16:18

The Church

Resistance is Futile

I love Star Trek. Maybe you do, maybe you don't. One of my favorite things is the Borg. The Borg, an alien species, travels around the universe collecting people. For most of the multi-faceted series, the Borg are evil (spoiler alert, they become nice). But nice or evil, the Borg's approach to conquering the universe is smart. They assimilate new species and cultures into their collective. During their evil days, they would approach a new species and announce, "We are the Borg. You will be assimilated. Resistance is futile." Then they would conquer the species and make them part of the collective. Each assimilation made the Borg smarter as the good traits and knowledge of the new species was added and shared among all the Borg. Ingenious!

I used to use the Borg as a picture of what it meant to be part of the the church, the collective of people who follow God. But my illustration always broke down because the Borg were evil. They killed those who resisted. Those that got assimilated became mindless drones. They were not saving the universe. They were destroying it.

But in the latest Star Trek release, Picard, the Borg change their ways. They are one of the good guys. They save people, prevent disasters, and allow people to choose whether to be part of the Borg. They are still unstoppable with each assimilation making them stronger. They still literally share one mind, one leader, and one goal. But now, they even help others who don't want to become Borg. They are out to save the universe.

For me, the Borg are a picture of what church really is. Church is not a building; it is a collective of people. When Jesus said, "I will build my church," he was not building a building or starting a program. Jesus was and is building an army to save the world and strengthen the saved. Every person has a gift, a strength, and a role. Each addition makes the church stronger, better, and more capable. Church is not a safe place; church is a strong people. People committed to God's ways and work. People committed to be better together. People committed to follow Jesus. People surrendered to God and each other for the common good. People who live in harmony and peace.

I love Jesus' view of his church when he says, "Not even the gates of hell can stand against my church." I can hear him saying to the lost and the evil, "We are the Church. Prepare to be assimilated. Resistance is futile. Love wins in the end. Evil loses. Choose well and be assimilated into something so strong and beautiful that you will never be the same." Becoming a follower of God is optional but have no doubt, Jesus' church, the one he builds, will defeat evil. Jesus' church is powerful to stand, to grow, to take care of each other, and to save the world. It is not a place. It is a people. The people of God. Now that is a church that I want to be a part of!

QUICK, SMART START

WHAT IS THE CHURCH?

One part of the will of God is that he will build His church. Jesus said,

> I will build my church, and all the powers of hell will not conquer it.
>
> Matthew 16:18

From the moment we put our faith in Christ, other Christians encourage us to attend church. They do so with good reason. The Bible is clear that Christians should gather together and become the complete "body of Christ" (see Romans 12:5). Christians need each other. We are designed to live in community. And history shows the children of God naturally gathering together.

Community with other believers provides strength when we are weak, a celebration when we praise, wisdom when we are young, and camaraderie in the battle. Not even hell itself can stand against or conquer the church. There is power in God's design of Christian community. But what is the church?

Have you ever heard someone brag about their church? They say things like:

- "My church is awesome,"
- "Our worship team is awesome. You should come to our church,"
- "Our pastor is an incredible teacher,"
- "Our church has an incredible children's worship center,"
- "Our church is beautiful. You should see the foyer," or,
- "Our church is involved in the community."

When people tell you what they like about their church, they most often tell you about things: programs, buildings, and bands. But have you ever heard someone complain about their church or the church they went to? The statements are revealing. You hear comments like,

- "Church is boring,"
- "My church didn't accept me,"
- "The pastor was always looking down on me,"

Romans 12:5 ESV

So we, though many, are one body in Christ, and individually members one of another.

- "All they talk about is money,"
- "They are hypocrites," or,
- "I don't fit in."

People like their church for many reasons; people seem to leave the church and hate the church for one main reason — the people. Without a doubt, the complainers could be wrong. But the complaints still cut through the clutter, revealing an important truth: the church is people.

1) What do you like best about your church? Do you like the place, the programs, or the people?

_____

_____

> *Church is not about the place; it is about the people.*

Church is not about the place; it is about the people. When Jesus said,

> I will build my church ...

he was not speaking of a physical building. He was not talking about a specific community. He was speaking metaphorically. Jesus was going to build (and is still building) a community of God-followers. He was not saying, "I am going to build the First Church of Jerusalem." Much like the will of God, Jesus was referring to the big picture when he said, "I will build my church." He was talking about every believer, everywhere throughout the ages.

Have you ever seen the word church capitalized like a proper name? Christian writers do this to identify the big picture church. Statements like "The Church needs to be the light to the world" could be rephrased, "All of the believers, everywhere need to be the light." The Church is bigger than any single location. The Church is bigger than any single gathering.

The Church is the entire community of people who worship the one true, living God. The Church is everyone who believes in Jesus Christ. The Church is everyone who is saved, who is forgiven. It is not a denomination, religion, or particular group. Paul reminded believers,

> God has put all things under the authority of Christ and has made him head over all things for the benefit of the church. And

> the church is his body; it is made full and complete by Christ, who fills all things everywhere with himself.
>
> Ephesians 1:22-23

The Church is made up of all the believers. The New Testament refers to the church as the "body of Christ" (see 1 Corinthians 10:17, Ephesians 4:12, Colossians 1:24). In the big picture, it is one body fitted together with one set of beliefs. God's design is one Church built by Jesus and united in one faith.

The Church is everyone who is saved, who is forgiven. It is not a denomination, religion, or particular group.

But, sadly, churches compete. Churches try to distinguish themselves from other churches. Churches band together around their particular beliefs forming denominations (specific divisions) of churches. The competition and division can be terribly confusing to unbelievers. Jesus said that he was building one Church. Paul emphasized this to a local church, one part of Jesus' Church,

> The human body has many parts, but the many parts make up one whole body. So it is with the body of Christ. Some of us are Jews, some are Gentiles, some are slaves, and some are free. But we have all been baptized into one body by one Spirit, and we all share the same Spirit.
>
> 1 Corinthians 12:13

Colossians 1:24

I am glad when I suffer for you in my body, for I am participating in the sufferings of Christ that continue for his body, the church.

The Church that Jesus is building is a community united in one faith, one Savior, one God, and one Spirit. His Church is, by definition, the entire community of believers. Every Christian is part of His church.

Can you imagine the power of the Church if all the local churches united under one faith in one God and one Savior? Can you imagine how the Church could save the world if we lived like one body, united and filled with one Spirit? What would the world see? They would see Jesus. And they would experience the power of God that he wants them to experience. He said,

> I will build my church, and all the powers of hell will not conquer it.
>
> Matthew 16:18

Jesus' church is the global community of all who believe in and follow Him.

2 Take a minute to review your memory verse for this week. Write it below.

_____

_____

_____

WHAT IS THE LOCAL CHURCH?

Day 2

The Church is the community of all those who believe in God. But, the Bible also records the history of the specific churches. Paul writes to the community of believers in Corinth. Peter writes to the churches scattered throughout the world. These specific churches are referred to as local churches — segments of the Church overall.

The local church is a group of people who have been saved and baptized, and gather together. They gather to worship, learn, and serve God in a specific area or place. In the New Testament, churches did not have their own fancy names. The local communities of believers were referred to as "the church." If Christians gathered in Corinth, they were referred to as the Church in Corinth (notice the big C). The churches in Galatia were called the Church in Galatia. The first gathering of believers was simply the Church in Jerusalem. Luke documented the early days of this new community.

> Those who believed what Peter said were baptized and added to the church that day—about 3,000 in all. All the believers devoted themselves to the apostles' teaching, and to fellowship, and to sharing in meals (including the Lord's Supper, and to prayer.
>
> A deep sense of awe came over them all, and the apostles performed many miraculous signs and wonders. And all the believers met together in one place and shared everything they had. They sold their property and possessions and shared the money with those in need.

They worshiped together at the Temple each day, met in homes for the Lord's Supper, and shared their meals with great joy and generosity—all the while praising God and enjoying the goodwill of all the people. And each day the Lord added to their fellowship those who were being saved.

Acts 2:41-47

Do you see it? They did not have a building. In fact, they met at the Jewish Temple for worship. They saw themselves as Jews who had met Jesus. They were a community of people not bound by the walls of a building. They met in homes, they met in parks, and they met at the Jewish temple. They were the Church all over Jerusalem! When Paul taught the local church in Rome, he reminded them that they were the body of Christ. When he led the local church in Corinth, he expanded the idea that the church is not a place or thing.

Now you are the body of Christ, and individual members of it.

1 Corinthians 12:27 HCSB

❸ Take a minute and read 1 Corinthians 12:12-27 below. Look for how Paul compares the Christians' community (or body) to the human body. Circle the word "body" each time you see it. Underline any phrase that talks about members or parts of the body.

For just as the body is one and has many members, and all the members of the body, though many, are one body, so it is with Christ. ¹³For in one Spirit we were all baptized into one body—Jews or Greeks, slaves or free—and all were made to drink of one Spirit.

¹⁴For the body does not consist of one member but of many. ¹⁵If the foot should say, "Because I am not a hand, I do not belong to the body," that would not make it any less a part of the body. ¹⁶And if the ear should say, "Because I am not an eye, I do not belong to the body," that would not make it any less a part of the body. ¹⁷If the whole body were an eye, where would be the

sense of hearing? If the whole body were an ear, where would be the sense of smell? ¹⁸But as it is, God arranged the members in the body, each one of them, as he chose. ¹⁹If all were a single member, where would the body be? ²⁰As it is, there are many parts, yet one body.

²¹The eye cannot say to the hand, "I have no need of you," nor again the head to the feet, "I have no need of you." ²²On the contrary, the parts of the body that seem to be weaker are indispensable, ²³and on those parts of the body that we think less honorable we bestow the greater honor, and our unpresentable parts are treated with greater modesty, ²⁴which our more presentable parts do not require. But God has so composed the body, giving greater honor to the part that lacked it, ²⁵that there may be no division in the body, but that the members may have the same care for one another. ²⁶If one member suffers, all suffer together; if one member is honored, all rejoice together. ²⁷Now you are the body of Christ and individually members of it.

> **Acts 2:41**
>
> Those who believed what Peter said were baptized and added to the church that day —about 3,000 in all.

Each local church is a body of Christ, a community of Christians that are interdependent on one another by God's design.

- Each member has a different function, verses 14-20.
- No one member can function alone, verse 21.
- Each member's contribution is essential, verses 22-24.
- A properly functioning body operates as a single unit, verses 25-27.

Jesus builds his church. Jesus adds to his church. Anyone who believes in Jesus is part of the Church (see **Acts 2:41**). Local churches are the communities, the bodies of God-followers that gather together locally.

QUICK, SMART START

4 One of the most incredible things about the Church in Jerusalem was that people saw God working miraculously through the people. As a result, thousands became Christians and part of the church. Where do you see God moving in your church?

_____

_____

_____

WHAT DO I DO IN THE CHURCH?

Sometimes the best way to figure out what to do is to learn from others' experiences. The New Testament records the history of the local churches. You can see what they did well and did not do well through their successes and failures. Earlier you read about the first local church, the church in Jerusalem (see Acts 2:41-47).

5 Below is a list of what they did together. Underline the items that your church does together.

- They baptized the new believers in Jesus, verse 41
- They taught and learned the Word of God, verse 42
- They fellowshipped with other believers, verse 42
- They prayed together, verse 42
- They ate together, verse 42
- They shared in the Lord's supper, verse 42
- They were a living testimony of God's grace and power, verse 43
- They helped each other and shared all their belongings, verse 44
- They sold their possessions to help those in need, verse 45
- They worshipped together in front of the world, verse 46
- They reached out to the community, verse 47, and
- They led people to salvation, verse 47.

Church leaders use this example as a template for what the church should do. They set up ministries to champion each goal, attempting to get the same spiritual result. They believe that the model will work if you work the model.

What so many miss is that the church in Jerusalem had no idea what they were doing. They were all new believers. There was no model. They gathered together because they wanted to learn more. They gathered together because they were part of the body of Christ. They gathered together around one simple, common belief. They were people who believed in Jesus Christ and His saving power. And as they gathered, they began to live out the teachings of Jesus together.

They did not worship to be the church. They worshipped because they loved God. They did not share their possessions because the church should share. They shared because people had needs and lived as a community. They did not evangelize because they should. They shared the message because they were passionate. They did not set out to do something they were supposed to do. They gathered together because they were Christians. What they did was the natural result of who they were.

So what should you do in the church? You should be a follower. You should be a teammate. You should be a Christian living out your faith with other Christians. You should worship with others the same way you worship alone. You should learn with others the same way you learn on your own. What you do in church, when you gather, will happen naturally as you follow God with other believers. God will use your spiritual gifts to strengthen the body of Christ, the church. And he will use the gifts of others to make you stronger.

As a community grows, some things need to get done. Someone has to teach. Someone has to serve. Someone has to make disciples. As you grow spiritually, you will want to help. But be careful not to make church about doing. That is one of the most significant errors of the modern church. Focus on experiencing God, worshipping God, and following God with others. Serve where needed. Use your talents and gifts but do what you do to build one another up instead of taking care of the building.

> *Use your talents and gifts but do what you do to build one another up instead of taking care of the building.*

QUICK, SMART START

6 Where has God led you to serve in your local church? Do you enjoy doing and being your part of the body of Christ? Write your answers below.

_____

_____

_____

_____

DO I NEED TO JOIN A CHURCH?

Churches that vote will require you to join in voting. Other churches use membership to create commitment and connection. They believe it helps people stay involved in the church. But, if you understand the Church biblically, you have to ask, "Why join a church when God has already made you a part of the Church?"

Membership in the local church is something governed by man. People have added requirements to being a part of their churches. God's only prerequisite is faith. If you are a Christian, you are a member of His Church. Shouldn't that be enough for local churches?

Local churches are just smaller communities of Jesus' Church. If the only requirement of God is faith, why do churches add requirements to be part of their church? Most Christian leaders have good intentions as they attempt to qualify church members.

- They are striving for unity and combatting division and problems.
- They are trying to make sure the people who want to join churches are living for Christ.
- They are trying to ensure that new members do not hold strange or unbiblical doctrines.

- If their church runs democratically where members vote on decisions, they often add requirements to ensure voters have the same beliefs and values.
- They want people to be committed to the church with the hopes that commitment will result in involvement.

Well-intentioned or not, when we add requirements, we suffer from the delusion of control. Churches have fought and split despite efforts to limit and control membership. Wrong people do wrong regardless of the rules. Control is an illusion; if you remove that illusion, there remains little reason to add any restriction other than faith in Jesus Christ.

A more modern idea of membership is a partnership. Churches encourage people to become partners in the local church. These churches are looking for long-term commitment before they let people lead, teach, and guide others. These churches want you to give consistently, attend regularly, and serve well. Again, you need to be understanding. Churches are just trying to figure out who is all in. But, this model has a significant flaw too. Why not just watch for those that are committed and build them towards leadership and service? Why not teach about the importance of commitment and then recognize those who are all in?

There is no biblical command for you to join a local church. You do not need to meet a set of requirements to be part of a church. No one should ask more of you than Jesus asks. But, you should definitely be committed to a local church. You need to be part of a healthy, thriving community. Christianity is best played as a team sport where each person strengthens every other person. Paul put it this way,

> There are different kinds of spiritual gifts, but the same Spirit is the source of them all. There are different kinds of service, but we serve the same Lord. God works in different ways, but it is the same God who does the work in all of us. A spiritual gift is given to each of us so we can help each other.
> 1 Corinthians 12:4-7

In the same way that a man and a woman complete each other, Christians make up the complete body of Christ. Complimenting strengths make the whole stronger than any of the individuals. This is the power of community. Paul taught another church the same truth explaining,

> Now these are the gifts Christ gave to the church: the apostles, the prophets, the evangelists, and the pastors and teachers. Their responsibility is to equip God's people to do his work and build up the church, the body of Christ. This will continue until we all come to such unity in our faith and knowledge of God's Son that we will be mature in the Lord, measuring up to the full and complete standard of Christ.
>
> Then we will no longer be immature like children. We won't be tossed and blown about by every wind of new teaching. We will not be influenced when people try to trick us with lies so clever they sound like the truth. Instead, we will speak the truth in love, growing in every way more and more like Christ, who is the head of his body, the church. He makes the whole body fit together perfectly. As each part does its own special work, it helps the other parts grow, so that the whole body is healthy and growing and full of love.
>
> Ephesian 4:11-16

Matthew 18:19

I also tell you this: If two of you agree here on earth concerning anything you ask, my Father in heaven will do it for you. For where two or three gather together as my followers, I am there among them.

As the local church gathers, it builds up, teaches, and strengthens individual believers. Each believer invests in other believers. Everyone makes disciples, and the whole community becomes robust. Whenever believers gather together, everyone grows stronger. You cannot experience all that God wants for you outside of community. Being part of a local church community is what God wants for you. There is power when we gather (see **Matthew 18:19**).

The teacher of the Hebrew believers instructed them,

> Let us hold tightly without wavering to the hope we affirm, for God can be trusted to keep his promise. Let us think of ways to motivate one another to acts of love and good works. And let us not neglect our meeting together, as some people do, but encourage one another, especially now that the day of his return is drawing near.
>
> Hebrews 10:23-25

God always draws his people together for their own good. You do not need to join a church, but you need to be part of a local church. You need community, and the community needs you. Community is God's design for his people.

7 Is your church improving you?

_____

How is it cheering you on and building up your faith?

_____

_____

Are there any areas you can pray that God will improve in your local church?

_____

_____

_____

WHERE SHOULD I GO TO CHURCH?

Day 5

The best place to start is by gathering with the people (the church) that led you to Christ or got you back to Christ. It makes sense. These people reached out to you. God used them. Your connection with them is your starting point with God.

For centuries, the question about where to go to church was quickly answered. Local churches were a function of geography. Society was not very mobile, and people gathered with Christians who lived nearby. With the growth of denominations (Baptist, Methodist, etc.), believers faced a new question: "Which church in my community should I go to?" In other words, "What brand of church should I attend?" Many went to the church that reached them for Christ. Others tried all the churches and picked the one they liked best. Others looked for the church with the best music or the best teaching. Choosing a church seemed to be a deeply personal thing.

People could venture to nearby towns and cities as society grew more mobile. The pool of available churches grew. Opportunities to experience different communities of believers grew. But, the challenge of figuring out what church to attend became larger as well.

With the rise of the large regional churches, people began driving long distances to attend church. The pool of churches grew larger. The opportunity to learn from teachers previously unavailable grew. There were more opportunities for involvement and personal growth. Again, the challenge of picking a church increased.

Then, the church went virtual. Christians began gathering across the nation or nations for worship and teaching. The possibilities for gathering grew and the question, "Where should I go to church?" became more challenging.

Theoretically, you should be able to go to any church where believers gather to walk with Christ. But, you might want to be aware of some of the common challenges among all these opportunities.

Believers in regional churches may find it challenging to be an active part of the church. They simply live too far away. Most large churches host smaller, local groups. But, only forty percent of attenders get involved. God designed his church to be interactive. Spiritual growth and discipleship happen best in real life. You may find it difficult to be challenged, accountable, and build relationships when you live far away.

Churches that primarily focus on weekly worship face the same challenge. It is challenging to be the body of Christ when the arms and legs are only together on Sundays.

It is easy to disappear in larger churches. Being a part of the crowd is actually attractive to many people. But, disappearing into the crowd is not helpful to spiritual growth and Christian living. Christianity is a team sport. If you tend to disappear easily, large churches may not be your best gathering place.

Smaller churches can wear people out. Small cannot do what big does. There are simply not enough people and resources to sustain the same level of opportunities. If you are an involvement addict, you need to be careful when picking a smaller church. Busy is not conducive to worship, learning, and spirituality.

Whatever church you attend, you need to be an active part of that mini-body of believers. You need to walk with the other Christians.

8 Is your church big or small, local or regional, online or in person?

_____

Are you actively involved in your church?

_____

Do you feel like a team member?

_____

Are you facing burnout?

_____

How will you overcome the challenges and be a healthy, active member of the body of Christ?

_____

_____

_____

_____

Whatever church you attend, you need to be an active part of that mini-body of believers. You need to walk with the other Christians. You need to be available to bear their burdens and develop deep relationships. You need to learn, and you need to share. Living life with the people in your church allows you to reap the benefits of community. Only time and exposure will allow you to develop the trust, transparency, and tenacity that helps you and them to be refined and purified.

God may want you to go to a specific church. He may want you in a place that makes you a bit uncomfortable so that you will grow. He may want you to help move a church closer to Him. Picking a church is not just about what you like or want. You should involve God in your decision. Remember, God has a much higher plan, and he might want to use you in a specific way in one particular church.

As you search for the answer to this question, keep these key factors fresh in your mind:

- Are the believers leading other believers to the Lord?
- Do they believe and teach the Bible as the Word of God and the infallible guide for life?
- Do they teach opinion and man's thoughts or the Bible?
- Is the focus on the leaders following God or everyone following God?
- Are the people encouraged to read and study the Bible as much as the leadership?
- Do the people serve the community?
- Are the people transparent, or are they plastic?
- Does the church help people to become prepared, confident, and skilled at living life with God?

9 Take a minute and write out your memory verse.

_____

_____

_____

_____

10 In your own words, what is the purpose of this lesson?

_____

_____

_____

_____

_____

AT THE END OF THE WEEK ANSWER THESE QUESTIONS

What was the most meaningful statement(s) or scripture this week?

_____
_____
_____
_____
_____
_____

Reword the statement or scripture into a prayer of response to God.

_____
_____
_____
_____
_____
_____

What actions do you need to take in response to this week's study?

_____
_____
_____
_____
_____
_____

TRUTH 9

MEMORY VERSE

For you are all children of God through faith in Christ Jesus. And all who have been united with Christ in baptism have put on Christ, like putting on new clothes. There is no longer Jew or Gentile, slave or free, male and female. For you are all one in Christ Jesus.

Galatians 3:26-28

Other Christians

Better Together, Always

Jesus is building an army to save the world and strengthen the saved. His Church is a collective of like-minded followers of God. Each addition makes the Church stronger, better, and more capable. And the local church, your and my immediate community of believers is a micro-view of God's bigger collective. A community committed to being better together. A community surrendered to God and to each other for the common good. People who live in harmony and peace.

But, harmony and peace take a bit of work. Being better together takes adjustment to and understanding each other. When we see each other the way God sees us and respect one another, the whole becomes more powerful than the sum of its parts. More powerful to follow God. More powerful to serve. More powerful to thrive. We are not just more powerful together. We also become more powerful, more refined, and stronger individually. This is the story of my journey too.

My life is so much better, clearer, and refined because of the Christians around me. I am not dependent on them to thrive or survive. Not at all! God can work through me completely. He has a plan for me. But as I thrive in my Christian life and surround myself with other thriving Christians, God makes me better. And he makes all of us better together than we would be alone.

Sure, there are bumps, misunderstandings, and times when we get frustrated. I experience this a lot. I am a creative thinker and, really, a bit odd. It seems I am always thinking about six things at once. I love to solve problems, so I ask a lot of questions. I value transparency, so I say what I think. When I connect with new people, it takes time for them to figure me out. I have to apologize for interrupting until they realize my brain is simply working too fast. I have to explain when I think aloud or drift off from conversations. My superpower is connecting the dots and solving problems. But my superpower can create some bumps until you know me.

It is the same with other people. I have to be patient. I have to get to know the back story of new community members to understand their reactions. I have to risk investing in their growth as they risk investing in mine. I have to figure out how they think. You get it. We have all been there.

Living with other Christians requires we believe God knows what he is doing. Living well with other Christians demands we adjust to God's view of community. He sees all of us the same. He values each and every one of us. He has a plan to take all our uniqueness and make each of us more complete. We must believe that each new addition to the family is essential to our completeness. When I do these things when I believe these things, the bumps along the way are well worth the incredible outcome. God is at work in us and around us as we live together well.

QUICK, SMART START

LIVING WITH OTHER CHRISTIANS

You became part of the Church Jesus is building when you became a Christian. You became a member of the "body of Christ." And, you joined a new family. Spiritually, you now have many new brothers and sisters. Every follower, with all their strengths and weaknesses, is your sibling. We all have the same Father, the same inheritance, and the same older brother — Jesus. (see Hebrews 2:11). Our spiritual family is not a word picture or a metaphor. It is a real family established by God.

> God knew them before He made the world, and He chose them to be like his Son so that Jesus would be the firstborn of many brothers and sisters.
>
> Romans 8:29 NCV

Hebrew 2:11

So now Jesus and the ones he makes holy have the same Father. That is why Jesus is not ashamed to call them his brothers and sisters.

 Who is "them" in the verse above?

_____

"Them" is anyone who believes in God the Father and his son, Jesus Christ. "They" are all part of God's family. The Christian life becomes a team effort as believers gather and live life together. Believers mature as they share their gifts, talents, skills, and resources. Individuals become stronger as everyone lives together in God's family (see Ephesians 4:16).

Ephesians 4:16

He makes the whole body fit together perfectly. As each part does its own special work, it helps the other parts grow, so that the whole body is healthy and growing and full of love.

But we are not always so good at gathering together. Relationships require trust, and relationships can be awkward. We bring all that we are, the good and the bad, and all the baggage from our former life into each new relationship. We are all still growing, and our need to improve can sometimes be annoying. It can be challenging to be patient and kind and to set aside our expectations and assumptions. But living closely with other believers is God's unique design for his family. God expects us to get along because he knows we can. He wants us to be patient with Christians who are different. God knows that their differences make us stronger. He tells us not to judge, to be forgiving, and to accept everyone the way they are. God's standard for relationships is unconditional love. He expects us to treat Christians as brothers and sisters.

Adjusting to God's expectations may be the most challenging work for Christian relationships. We all have an idea of what a healthy family should look like. Each of us has a mental picture of what a great big brother or little sister should be like. And each of us has our own reality, which often falls short of the ideal. We have expectations, and adjusting those expectations to God's expectations can be challenging. But when we adjust to God's design for living together, we can experience the power of being the family of God.

ALL CHRISTIANS ARE EQUAL

Day 2

Every Christian -- regardless of age, creed, or nationality -- is your brother or sister. We have one Father and one Savior, and one Spirit. All of us are the children of God. There is no greater and no lesser. Some brothers are older, but they are still brothers and not fathers. Some sisters are wiser and more intelligent, but they are still sisters and not better. We are all children of God.

> The Father has loved us so much that we are called children of God. And we really are his children. The reason the people in the world do not know us is that they have not known him. Dear friends, now we are children of God, and we have not yet been shown what we will be in the future. But we know that when Christ comes again, we will be like him, because we will see him as he really is.
>
> 1 John 3:1-2 NCV

Every Christian has the same standing, rights, privileges, and responsibilities. You should not respect one person more than another. You should not elevate your leaders above those who follow alongside you. There is no social-cast system for Christians. We are brothers and sisters of Jesus. We are children of God. Embracing this equality is essential when you follow and when you lead.

Unfortunately, many churches create a leadership class by giving their leaders titles like bishop or father. Others insist on using titles like pastor, shepherd, and reverend out of respect for their leaders. Unfortunately, terms like these make a distinction between Christians that God never makes. Jesus said,

> They (the religious leaders in Jesus' time) love the place of honor at banquets, the front seats in the synagogues, greetings in the marketplaces, and to be called 'Rabbi' by people.
>
> But as for you, do not be called 'Rabbi,' because you have one Teacher, and you are all brothers. Do not call anyone on earth your father, because you have one Father, who is in heaven. And do not be called masters either, because you have one Master, the Messiah. The greatest among you will be your servant. Whoever exalts himself will be humbled, and whoever humbles himself will be exalted.
>
> Matthew 23:8-12 HCSB

When it comes to the family of God, distinctions between leaders and followers are unbiblical. How has the church missed this? Leaders that need a title oppose and ignore Jesus' teaching. Mature leaders are humble. They are comfortable with their low status compared to the King. Mature leaders are broken, honest, and give all the honor to God. They embrace the equality of their brothers and sisters in Christ. But immature churches and leaders are not the only ones who make distinctions of equality.

Followers also settle into the same spiritual class systems. Church members often treat leaders differently. Some fear them. Some put them at the front of the line. And many followers expect their leaders to be perfect or, at least, better. We even elevate one leader above the other. It seems we just have to put people on pedestals. The believers in Corinth made this error when they picked their favorite leaders. Paul responded,

> So, what is Apollos? And what is Paul? They are servants through whom you believed, and each has the role the Lord has given. I planted, Apollos watered, but God gave the growth. So then neither the one who plants nor the one who waters is anything, but only God who gives the growth. Now the one who plants and the one who waters are equal, and each will receive his own reward according to his own labor. For we are God's co-workers. You are God's field, God's building.
>
> 1 Corinthians 3:5-9 HCSB

"Only God gives the growth" is a crucial concept in Paul's argument. We do many things, but God builds his Church. God saves. God redeems. God forgives. Paul is clear. We are all equal. Some lead and some follow, but we are all equal in the family of God. Even our leaders are all equal. We are the children of God, and we have one Father and one Lord. We do not need priests, fathers, pastors, or any person to manage our relationship with God.

> There is one God and one Mediator who can reconcile God and humanity—the man Christ Jesus.
> 1 Timothy 2:5

But, the danger of inequality is not limited to the issue of leadership. Our tendency to treat people differently is widespread. Our tendency to offer more respect to one person than another is epidemic in our flesh. James warns,

> My dear brothers and sisters, how can you claim to have faith in our glorious Lord Jesus Christ if you favor some people over others? For example, suppose someone comes into your meeting dressed in fancy clothes and expensive jewelry, and another comes in who is poor and dressed in dirty clothes. If you give special attention and a good seat to the rich person, but you say to the poor one, "You can stand over there, or else sit on the floor"—well, doesn't this discrimination show that your judgments are guided by evil motives?
>
> But if you favor some people over others, you are committing a sin. You are guilty of breaking the law.
> James 2:1-4,9

Peter tells Christian men living in a chauvinistic society to fix themselves and their culture.

> In the same way, you husbands must give honor to your wives. Treat your wife with understanding as you live together. She may be weaker than you are, but she is your equal partner in God's gift of new life. Treat her as you should so your prayers will not be hindered.
> 1 Peter 3:7

Jesus made it clear -- all believers are equal. Paul reiterated it time and time again. We are all children of God. We are all equals.

QUICK, SMART START

> For you are all children of God through faith in Christ Jesus. And all who have been united with Christ in baptism have put on Christ, like putting on new clothes. There is no longer Jew or Gentile, slave or free, male and female. For you are all one in Christ Jesus.
>
> Galatians 3:26-28

If you are going to get all the benefits of Christian relationships, you need to embrace the equality of believers. You need to let leaders be individual humans. You need to fight your tendency to treat people differently. You need to encourage others to find the beauty of being children, joint heirs, and siblings. We are not orphans. We are not alone. God has made us a family, and every relationship makes us more complete.

We need to set an excellent example as new believers become part of the family. We need to welcome them as equal partakers in the blessings of God. We need to champion God's ideal family and God's truths about Christian relationships. We need to live out and champion the equality of all believers.

❷ Write this week's memory verse and practice it out loud.

_____

_____

_____

ALL CHRISTIANS ARE DIFFERENT

Day 3

The variety of God's creation is visible. You see it in the thousands of species with all their crazy flair and skills. You see it in your garden. You see it when you travel. You see it in the people you meet. People come in all shapes and sizes: tall, short, skinny, less skinny, redheads, dirty blondes, strong, and weaker. Some people are emotional, while others are more clinical. We may be equal, but we are most definitely different.

We are introverts, extroverts, engineers, artists, and artisans. From our fingerprints to how we think, we are a mess of variety.

We are not only unique in personality and person; we are unique in spirit. Spiritual variety is part of God's design. The Holy Spirit gives different spiritual gifts to different believers. Paul explained it this way,

> There are different kinds of spiritual gifts, but the same Spirit is the source of them all. There are different kinds of service, but we serve the same Lord. God works in different ways, but it is the same God who does the work in all of us. A spiritual gift is given to each of us so we can help each other.
>
> 1 Corinthians 12:4-7

God loves variety, and his variety has a purpose. Instead of desiring Christians to be independent, he designed them to be interdependent. He created us to complete one another (see Lesson 8). God makes everyone different. He gives each of us different, complimenting gifts that come together and make a whole. Some believers are teachers, and others are good at encouraging. Some have financial wisdom, and some have unique spiritual insight. Some believers are good at details, and others see the big picture. You can find examples of God's unique spiritual gifts throughout the Bible (see Romans 12, 1 Corinthians 12). He even gives spiritual gifts that are very practical, like musical ability and craftsmanship (see Exodus 31:2-3). And he always uses those individual gifts to complete his work and mature his people. Paul used the human body as a word picture to explain this concept.

Exodus 31:2-3

I have specifically chosen Bezalel son of Uri, grandson of Hur, of the tribe of Judah. I have filled him with the Spirit of God, giving him great wisdom, ability, and expertise in all kinds of crafts.

❸ Read the passage below. Underline the words or phrases that stress the variety of God's design. Circle the words or phrases that emphasize the equality of believers.

> The human body has many parts, but the many parts make up one whole body. So it is with the body of Christ. Some of us are Jews, some are Gentiles, some are slaves, and some are free. But we have all been baptized into one body by one Spirit, and we all share the same Spirit.
>
> Yes, the body has many different parts, not just one part. If the foot says, "I am not a part of the body because I am not a hand," that does not make it any less a part of the body. And if the ear

says, "I am not part of the body because I am not an eye," would that make it any less a part of the body? If the whole body were an eye, how would you hear? Or if your whole body were an ear, how would you smell anything?

But our bodies have many parts, and God has put each part just where he wants it. How strange a body would be if it had only one part! Yes, there are many parts, but only one body. The eye can never say to the hand, "I don't need you." The head can't say to the feet, "I don't need you."

Variety with God's purpose is God's design!

In fact, some parts of the body that seem weakest and least important are actually the most necessary. And the parts we regard as less honorable are those we clothe with the greatest care. So we carefully protect those parts that should not be seen, while the more honorable parts do not require this special care. So God has put the body together such that extra honor and care are given to those parts that have less dignity. This makes for harmony among the members, so that all the members care for each other. If one part suffers, all the parts suffer with it, and if one part is honored, all the parts are glad.

1 Corinthians 12:12-26

Variety with purpose is God's design. But in all that variety, God stresses equality. He wants us to live as a complete spiritual ecosystem. You become complete by living well with other followers. Many relationships work to create the whole of God's family. But, this new life also brings new learning, challenges, and opportunity for growth.

There is a saying, "You can pick your friends but not your family." It's true with our biological families and with our spiritual family. You could pick and choose your friends before joining God's family. And, you probably picked friends with similar interests. Your relationships grew from shared experiences like work, baseball, or running. But now, God's most important relationships for you are family relationships. There is no picking and choosing. We are related.

 Who do you hang out with at church?

_____

5 Do you seem to gravitate to only people your age or people who share common interests?

_____

_____

6 What steps can you take to adjust to God's variety and improve your Christian community?

_____

_____

God has adopted us into his family. You are in the family, and you have a wide variety of brothers and sisters. If you are an introvert, you now have an unlimited number of extrovert, annoying, needy little brothers. If you are an extrovert, you have to figure out what to do with your new big sister, who processes quietly, leaving you wondering what she is thinking. The dreamers get to wrestle with their new analytical siblings, who seem to be party poopers. The list goes on and on. All of God's variety grows you, improves you, refines you, and makes you all that God wants you to be. It is God's incredible design.

Embracing and experiencing God's variety is powerful and necessary. If you only hang out with siblings like you, you will miss out on God's variety plan. Be proactive in building new relationships. Go to lunch with a spiritual sibling you do not usually hang out with. Sit with someone different during worship. Go on a mission trip and live with different brothers and sisters. Go to the park with someone older or younger. Take steps to share your unique you with everyone in the family. Embrace God's design.

> As each has received a gift, use it to serve one another, as good stewards of God's varied grace: whoever speaks, as one who speaks oracles of God; whoever serves, as one who serves by the strength that God supplies—in order that in everything God may be glorified through Jesus Christ. To him belong glory and dominion forever and ever. Amen.
> 1 Peter 4:10-11 ESV

All of us are equal. All of us are different. And all of us have responsibilities in our new spiritual family.

QUICK, SMART START

FAMILY RESPONSIBILITIES

Every earthly family has responsibilities. Every member has chores. Parents expect children to help one another. Great big brothers defend little brothers from bullies. Big sisters help carry science projects to school. Little brothers set up the slip and slide and beg everyone to come to have fun. Little sisters say the darnedest things to encourage sad big sisters. Your spiritual family is no different. You can and should be that great big brother or sister. You should be that helpful little brother or sister. The Bible is full of instructions on how we can come together to be much healthier, happier, and more successful than we could ever be alone.

 Below is a sampling from the New Testament. Write the family responsibility that you find next to the Bible verse.

a. 1 Thessalonians 1:2-3, 2 Timothy 1:3 _____

b. 1 John 3:17-18, Romans 12:13 _____

c. Acts 11:27-30 _____

d. Galatians 6:10 _____

e. Galatians 6:1-2; Romans 15:1-2 _____

f. 1 Thessalonians 5:11 _____

g. Philippians 2:3-4 _____

h. Matthew 20:25-28 _____

i. 1 John 3:14-16 _____

j. Ephesians 4:2 _____

k. James 5: 19-20 _____

l. Ephesians 4:32, Colossians 3:13 _____

We need to pray for our brothers and sisters (a). Almost every one of Paul's letters opens with a prayer for those he is writing, but you have a more specific target. You can make a list of the people in your direct spiritual family and pray for each of them daily or weekly. You may even want to ask them how you can pray for them. We need to meet our sibling's physical needs (b). The more you know, the more you can help. You need to extend this help to other ministries, churches, and believers not in your immediate family (c). Your goal should be to do good to everyone, especially to your family members (d). Christians should meet each other's spiritual needs by providing safety, restoration, and forgiveness (e). You need to encourage and lift up your brothers and sisters with words that improve them (f). You should practice humility that springs from understanding God's equality (g). You need to serve one another and, when you lead, practice servant leadership (h). You need to love your siblings in Christ well, sharing the love that God has given you (i). You must be patient (j) and rescue other Christians from error instead of abandoning or judging them (k). And, you need to provide compassion and forgive your siblings (l).

As you live this way with other believers, your family will grow and increase. All of you will become more mature, more complete, and more powerful to carry the love of Christ to the world. You will enjoy God's design, and the world will see his glory.

8 Take a minute and put a checkmark next to each of the family responsibilities you are currently doing. What responsibility are you best at?

HOW DO I HANDLE CONFLICTS WITH MY SPIRITUAL FAMILY?

Day 5

Experiencing God's variety brings blessings, but adjusting to the variety in others can also be a challenge. Some of the adjustments require you to stretch. Introverts need to embrace the beauty of extroverts. Detail-oriented believers quickly realize that dreamers are not like them. But, without a dreamer starting something new, there would be little for them to organize. The list of adjustments goes on and on but remember

> **Ephesians 4:26-27**
>
> And don't sin by letting anger control you. Don't let the sun go down while you are still angry, for anger gives a foothold to the devil.

that variety in the family is God's plan. Everyone is a valuable and necessary part of the body.

Adjustment does not have to bring conflict, but it often does. You will probably get offended at some point. A leader or friend will unwittingly push you too far too quickly. A brother or sister will mess up and do or say something that offends you. You might struggle with a spiritual family member who is not being part of the productive whole. You might get frustrated with your little brothers. Just like your physical family, there will be times of offense, hurt, and disagreement as we grow spiritually. But do not worry; the Bible gives us instructions on how to handle conflict.

First and foremost, if you get angry, do not let your anger control you. Anger is a God-given emotion, but you need to be careful not to sin when you get angry, frustrated, or discouraged. Anger may point to a needed fix, but anger can quickly get out of control. We need to slow down, listen, and pray before we speak.

Second, resolve conflict quickly. (see **Ephesians 4:26-27**). After you think and pray, do not avoid the confrontation. Unresolved conflict is like cancer to the family of God. It divides, mutates, and destroys, worsening the longer it remains alive. You need to talk to the person who has made you feel anger, angst, hurt, or frustration. Ask them why they did what they did. Tell them how it made you feel. Listen to them. You may find that they did not mean what you heard. They may have reacted wrongly because of stress or exhaustion. You might find that you can help. You can leverage James' teaching as you talk about conflict.

> Understand this, my dear brothers and sisters: You must all be quick to listen, slow to speak, and slow to get angry. Human anger does not produce the righteousness God desires.
>
> James 1:19-20

Third, be transparent in conflict. Risk being honest and explaining what you are feeling. You might find that you are misreading or that the other party misspoke. Your friendships will deepen, your trust will grow, and God will be honored as his children live like a united, all-for-one, one-for-all family.

Fourth, no matter what you do, believe the best about your brothers and sisters in Christ. God does. He knows their potential. He knows your potential. Start from the perspective that you or they must have misunderstood or made a mistake. Believe that you can work things out and be better on the backend. Live the hope that God gives us in Christ. Never abandon your brothers and sisters.

When conflicts arise, it is vital to know God's plan for handling family conflicts. Below are a few Biblical tips when things go wrong with a brother or sister.

When something goes wrong.

- **Pray and check yourself** (see Matthew 7:3-5). Ask, "Could I be wrong?"
- **Calm down before handling conflict** (see James 1:19-20). My rule is to wait a minimum of 24 hours when I do not understand the conflict. But I never go more than 72 hours without trying to work through conflict.
- **Talk to your brother or sister and do it quickly and privately** (see Ephesians 4:26-27). My rule is a few minutes for family and close friends. The trust we share allows us to resolve things quickly.
- **Try to settle it between yourselves** (see Matthew 18:15). Always talk privately to the one who offended you, or you offended. Do not take others or get people involved unless you have to. Assume that God can work this out and go quietly and discreetly. Even if they are wrong, try to help them recover.
- Ask the other person to pray with you for God's help as you settle the misunderstanding.

When something cannot be resolved.

- **Accept that something has been done wrong** (see 1 Corinthians 6:7-8).
- **Do not take a civil problem to the lost world for resolution** (see 1 Corinthians 6:1-6).
- **Commit the situation to God and let it go** (see 1 Peter 2:19-23).
- **Forgive the person** (see Colossians 3:13).
- **Pray for the person** (see Matthew 5:43-48; Romans 12:14)

There are times when it may help to get someone else involved. You might want to reach out to a mentor to think about the problem before you try to resolve it. If you are going to reach out for third-party help,

> **Matthew 18:17**
>
> If the person still refuses to listen, take your case to the church. Then if he or she won't accept the church's decision, treat that person as a pagan or a corrupt tax collector.

pick someone wiser than you and the person you are in conflict with. Pick someone who knows the Bible and does not give opinions. Pick someone who understands how not to get involved. In rare cases, it may help to get someone to sit with both of you to help talk the conflict through. Be careful not to share or shame the other person in the process.

It can seem impossible to forgive someone who will not resolve a conflict or their part in it. But forgiveness is always possible. My brother was trying to help someone move on from a great offense done to her by another person. He asked, "How can she be expected to forgive when her offender doesn't admit his error?" I was stumped at first, but as I prayed and thought, God gave me an answer I did not expect. He gave me a definition of forgiveness that set me free. Forgiveness is saying, "You owe me nothing." It is the one-sided forgiveness that Jesus provided on the cross. He forgave all of us before we even asked for forgiveness. Jesus made a permanent way for us to reconcile with him. In essence, he said, "I have already dealt with this. I have paid for your sin. When and if you are ready, you can have this forgiveness that I already provided." When someone does not work things out, just decide to forgive them and move on. Resolve the matter. Extend the forgiveness you have received. One-sided, unconditional forgiveness will provide a way for them, but, more importantly, it will prevent bitterness in you. Sometimes you simply have to move on.

❾ Is there someone you have not forgiven, or you hold bitterness against? Write a prayer of forgiveness to God and set them and yourself free.

_____

_____

_____

_____

There are times when someone actually sins against you. There are times when people choose not to live as Christians. There are times when people walk away from God's truths and reconciliation. The Bible teaches us to treat these folks as unbelievers (see Matthew 18:17). Though some believe that means you put such people out of the church, I believe it simply means what it says. You may need to limit time with them, but do not exile them from the church. Treat them like an unbeliever — try to win them back to Christ.

Finally, be proactive and follow Jesus' advice.

> So if you are presenting a gift at the altar in the Temple and you suddenly remember that someone has something against you, leave your sacrifice there at the altar. Go and be reconciled to that person. Then come and offer your sacrifice to God.
> Matthew 5:23-24

If you think your spiritual sibling has an issue with you, stop what you are doing and go try to fix it, even if he is the one who did wrong. Work to live peaceably as a united spiritual family.

❿ Write and practice your memory verse below.

_____

_____

_____

AT THE END OF THE WEEK ANSWER THESE QUESTIONS

What was the most meaningful statement(s) or scripture this week?	Reword the statement or scripture into a prayer of response to God.	What actions do you need to take in response to this week's study?

TRUTH 10

MEMORY VERSE

For "Everyone who calls on the name of the Lord will be saved." But how can they call on him to save them unless they believe in him? And how can they believe in him if they have never heard about him? And how can they hear about him unless someone tells them?

Romans 10:13-14

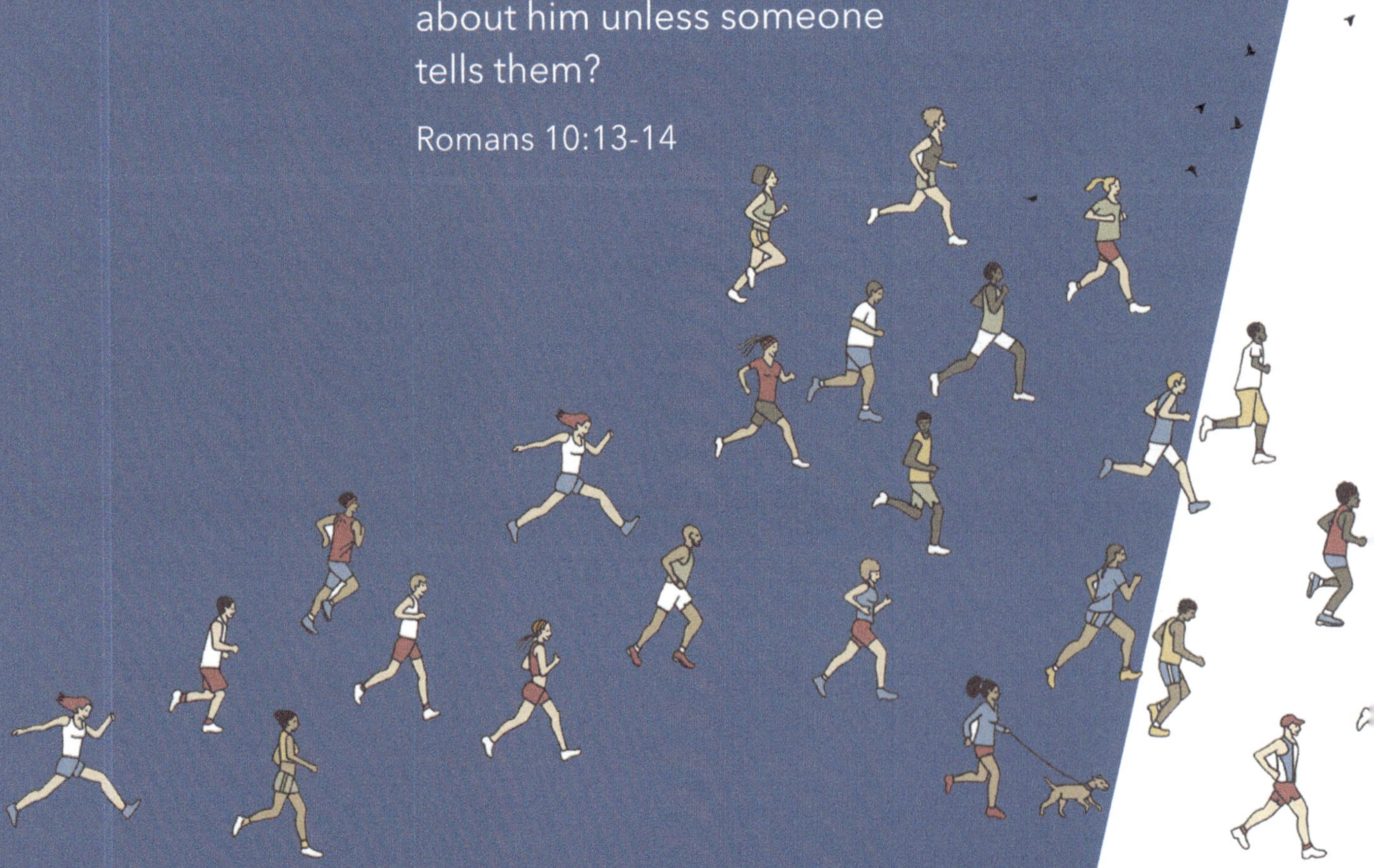

Living Among the World

Good Brings Opportunity

My wife and I moved twice in one year. The first move was from our small town outside Atlanta to a tiny apartment inside Atlanta. We moved from a big, old, beautiful house on the square to a tiny apartment. Then after seven months of waiting, we moved into our new suburban home in a small subdivision. Two moves. Three communities. And I noticed a trend.

There were two kinds of people in each community. Those that wanted to live there and those that wanted out. The ones that wanted to live there seemed to appreciate the blessing. The ones that wanted out seemed happy with nothing. Then I noticed something else.

The content and thankful people seemed to find favor. I guess it makes sense. We have all heard the saying, "You catch more flies with honey than vinegar." But the content and thankful people were not trying to catch flies. They were just well-balanced, good people living well where they were. In the small town, the ones who liked being there had friends, laughter, and shared in the light of the community. At the apartment, the ones who lived good, friendly lives got their maintenance requests done quicker and had friends next door. In the new construction community, the thankful found favor with the builder. They actually got served quicker and got perks they never asked for.

Amber and I were among the thankful, good living group. It's not that we are fantastic people. It's just that we are grateful to have what we have. God has blessed us so much. We are committed to following God and living peacefully. We want to be understanding and help others - because it is right and because it is fun. And, like the rest of the content group, we found favor in all three communities. We were missed by the ones we left. We are accepted at the one we now call home. The people compliment us and thank us for being kind. Our builder tells us again and again how thankful he is for homeowners that are patient and think the best about him.

Amber and I have seen this in our lives and other people's lives too. Living good brings blessings. And it also brings opportunity. We love telling people the good news about why we live the way we live. Sharing God's love and his plan is even easier when people notice your good life. Good brings the opportunity to share God's love with the world. You shouldn't live good lives just to share, but if you live good lives, you will always get to share. The world is looking for love even when they don't know it.

QUICK, SMART START

YOU ARE DIFFERENT

Your life changed when you committed to being a disciple of Jesus. Your values began to shift towards God's values. You live in the same world, but you are increasingly different. As God continues to convince you of a better way to live, your decisions and actions will continue to change. Peter described it as living like a foreigner or alien on this earth.

> Dear friends, I warn you as "temporary residents and foreigners" to keep away from worldly desires that wage war against your very souls. Be careful to live properly among your unbelieving neighbors. Then even if they accuse you of doing wrong, they will see your honorable behavior, and they will give honor to God when he judges the world.
>
> 1 Peter 2:11-12

Living among the world allows God to continue to live on earth as He lives through you.

You will succeed as you become more prepared, skilled, and confident at following God. Your emotions will even out. Your peace will increase. Your life will become more complete. There is no doubt that you will intentionally and unintentionally share your success, joy, and hope with those around you.

You are a citizen of heaven, but you live among people who are still citizens of earth. And they will begin to notice the change in you. Some people will cheer you on. Some will push back and want you to be the old you. Other people may even persecute you for the change in your beliefs, values, and actions. And some people will see your better life and begin to ask questions.

Living among the world can be challenging. It can be awkward to feel like an oddball with old friends. You may face internal and external pressures to do things the old way. If you used to cut corners at work, your boss or workers might have a problem with your desire to now do things the right way. If your spouse is not a believer, your faith may upset, convict, or inconvenience them.

There is no getting around the challenges of living among the people of the old world as a new person. But, living among the world allows God to continue to live on earth as He lives through you. You can live a balanced, consistent Christian life among this world.

 Write this week's memory verse in the margin.

DO I NEED TO CHANGE FRIENDS?

Day 2

If you had cancer and discovered a cure for cancer, would you abandon your chemotherapy friends or share the cure? You would share the cure. You know what they are facing. You know the pain. You know the hopelessness of cancer. You would do anything in your power to save them! You would give them the pill. They would take it.

There is absolutely no reason to dump your old friends. In fact, there is every reason to keep them. One of the most significant opportunities you have is to let your new life rub off on your old friends. You have the cure to death and empty living. Who better to share it with than your friends? Without a doubt, having cancer is different than not knowing God. When you have cancer, you know that without a cure, you will die. But, most people do not know that they are dying without God. It might take time for them to see that you are "healed" of your old, empty life. It might take time for them to see that they are dying spiritually. Your new life is light in the darkness. Your new life can help them see that they are dying without God. And when they begin to understand (just like you did!), many will take the cure.

Paul wrote these words to encourage the Romans to share the cure with their friends and world,

> Everyone who calls on the name of the Lord will be saved. But how can they call on him to save them unless they believe in him? And how can they believe in him if they have never heard about him? **And how can they hear about him unless someone tells them?** And how will anyone go and tell them without being sent? That is why the Scriptures say, "How beautiful are the feet of messengers who bring good news!"
> Romans 10:13-15

You have an incredible gift that you can share with your friends – you can share your new life.

You have an incredible gift that you can share with your friends — you can share your new life. You can share your success. You can share your hope and peace. There is no reason to change friends when you get saved, but there are many reasons to live your changed life in front of them. But be prepared for your friendships to change. Your new life may convict your old friends. They may not invite you to parties. You will

QUICK, SMART START

There is no reason to change friends when you get saved, but there are many reasons to live your changed life in front of them.

become uncomfortable with their old behaviors. You may need to flee the temptations of your old way of living and find new ways to hang out with them.

 Do you need to change how or where you hang out with old friends to avoid temptation?

_____

_____

When you went head-over-heels for that new girl, did your old friends push back, saying, "Dude, you never do anything with the guys anymore! You're always with Sally." Your friends may do the same thing as you make new friendships at church or Bible study.

Now that you are in love with Jesus, you need to make time for your old friends just like you did when you fell in love with Sally. You need to stay available to them. You need to be there for them because they are your friends. Allow them to see the cure. When "super religious" people challenged Jesus for hanging out with sinners, he said,

1 Timothy 2:4

God wants everyone to be saved and to understand the truth.

John 6:44

For no one can come to me unless the Father who sent me draws them to me, and at the last day I will raise them up.

> Healthy people don't need a doctor—sick people do. I have come to call not those who think they are righteous, but those who know they are sinners.
>
> Mark 2:17

Jesus intentionally spent time with people who needed what he had. You have the same opportunity. Do not make them projects. Just love them, tell them the truth, and answer their questions. You can leverage your new life to give them new life. It is working for you, and it will work for them. Assume that they, like you, want a cure. Whatever you do, do not cut them off. You might be the only one who can save them. You might be the only one they will listen to. You are the best person to share salvation with your friends.

John 5:17

Jesus replied, "My Father is always working, and so am I."

So how do you know when to share? And how do you know who to share with? The obvious answer seems to be anyone, anytime, anywhere. But as Paul encouraged believers to share, he also reminded them not everyone is ready to listen (see Romans 10:16). Jesus told his disciples,

> If any household or town refuses to welcome you or listen to your message, shake its dust from your feet as you leave.
>
> Matthew 10:14

138

Clearly, some people are not ready to listen. But there are four principles you can leverage to find those who are ready.

1. God's will is that everyone be saved (see **1 Timothy 2:4**).
2. God is the one who draws people toward him (see **John 6:44**).
3. God is always at work (see **John 5:17**).
4. God wants you to join him in his process (see **Matthew 28:19-20**).

God is working to draw people to him because he wants them to be saved. You do not have to pressure people. You do not have to convince people. God is at work. He can and will draw people towards salvation -- even those who are not looking for him (see **Romans 10:20**). These are his words.

So let God do the drawing and just look for the people that he is drawing. Listen for people who ask you questions about your life. They want to know what you have. God is drawing them. Pay attention when your friends share their troubles. They are looking for answers. God is drawing them. When you see God working, drawing your friends, make time. Stop what you are doing or schedule a time to hang out. They are recognizing a need. They are talking to you. And you know the cure.

❸ List at least three people you think God could be drawing towards himself. How can you safely spend time and share Jesus with them?

_____

_____

You do not need to change friends, even if those friendships change. But embrace your new friendships too. Your new friends will become a critical part of your life as you follow Christ. They provide the same hope, peace, challenge, and camaraderie you are trying to share with your old friends.

❹ Make a list below of the new friends God is putting in your path. How can you make time to connect with them?

_____

_____

Matthew 28:19-20

go and make disciples of all nations, baptizing them in the name of the Father and of the Son and of the Holy Spirit, and teaching them to obey everything I have commanded you. And surely I am with you always, to the very end of the age.

Romans 10:20

I was found by people who were not looking for me. I showed myself to those who were not asking for me.

QUICK, SMART START

WHAT DO I DO WHEN PEOPLE PUSH BACK?

What do you do when people push back on your faith? Be nice.

People have been pushing back on Christianity for centuries. There is little doubt that someone will push back on your new faith. Friends and coworkers may not believe the change at first. They may point out hypocrisy as you accidentally sin or intentionally err. Old friends may push back because they miss the old you. They may push back because your new faith makes them question their way of life. New acquaintances may push back on the hope you share. Whatever the cause, there is no doubt that people will push back on your Christianity.

So, what do you do when people push back? Be nice. It is that simple. Be nice. No one listens to a bully. No one listens to defensive people. The writer of Proverbs wrote,

> A gentle answer deflects anger, but harsh words make tempers flare.
>
> Proverbs 15:1

Avoid controversy whenever you can. Live peacefully. Bring peace into potential debates. Instead of getting upset when people push back, accept that lost people do lost things. Accept that they do not understand. Remember, lost people do not even know that they are lost. Paul explained it this way,

> The devil who rules this world has blinded the minds of those who do not believe. They cannot see the light of the Good News—the Good News about the glory of Christ, who is exactly like God.
>
> 2 Corinthians 4:3-4

When people push back, be compassionate. Remember where you came from. Remember what it was like when you did not understand. Give simple answers that bring hope. Simply share your story. It is not your job to convince them. Convincing them is God's job. Quiet confidence is a superpower when sharing God's Good News.

But what do you do if someone intentionally tries to mess with your career, life, happiness, and success because of your faith? What do you do if someone attacks your character, gossips about you, or makes fun of your faith? Your enemy, the devil, would love nothing more than for you to get in a fight. The devil would love to see your old, self-righteous, angry self get in a brawl. He would love for you to be unloving!

> Control yourselves and be careful! The devil, your enemy, goes around like a roaring lion looking for someone to eat.
> 1 Peter 5:8

God is a God of peace, and when it comes to attacks on our faith, he encourages us to avoid fights. When you face direct opposition, fight with love. Return love and empathy for hurt and anger.

> Never pay back evil with more evil. Do things in such a way that everyone can see you are honorable. Do all that you can to live in peace with everyone.
> Romans 12:17-18

Confidence and understanding in times of conflict may not always defuse an angry opponent, but they definitely will stop the fight. People cannot fight you if you do not fight back. King Solomon encouraged people to go further than not fighting -- he encouraged them to bless their enemies.

> If your enemies are hungry, give them food to eat. If they are thirsty, give them water to drink. You will heap burning coals of shame on their heads, and the Lord will reward you.
> Proverbs 25:22

And Paul adds,

> Don't let evil conquer you, but conquer evil by doing good.
> Romans 12:21

Jesus never called us to be weak. He called us to be peacemakers. More often than not, your opponents will be the people most ready for salvation. Make sure you show opponents of your faith the better life you have found. This is why Peter reminds us to never stop living good lives in front of the the world (see **1 Peter 2:12**). In the end, good always wins, and people will recognize that Jesus changes lives for good.

---

1 Peter 2:12

Be careful to live properly among your unbelieving neighbors. Then even if they accuse you of doing wrong, they will see your honorable behavior, and they will give honor to God when he judges the world

QUICK, SMART START

Grace, empathy, and remaining faithful to God are your greatest strengths when people push back on your faith.

❺ Do you need to make any changes in how you handle conversations with those who do not believe? If so, write those changes as a prayer to God, asking for his help.

_____

_____

_____

_____

WHAT DO I DO WHEN MY FAMILY DOES NOT BELIEVE?

Some of the greatest opposition to salvation comes from our families. Your girlfriend, husband, or parents may not believe in God, and they might not believe you have changed. How do you live your new life when your family does not want to go on the journey with you? Peter gave this advice to women living in a chauvinistic world with unbelieving husbands.

> In the same way, you wives must accept the authority of your husbands. Then, even if some refuse to obey the Good News, your godly lives will speak to them without any words. They will be won over by observing your pure and reverent lives.
> 1 Peter 3:1-2

Peter recognized that women were not being treated as equals. He realized that their world was not fair. In fact, he wrote this to Christian husbands,

> In the same way, you husbands must give honor to your wives. Treat your wife with understanding as you live together.
> 1 Peter 3:7

142

Peter encouraged wives with unsaved husbands to go easy, show their faith, pray, and win their husbands with love, grace, and respect. God knows that men do not respond well to nagging! He told husbands to leave the world's system and respect their wives as equals, writing,

> ...she is your equal partner in God's gift of new life. Treat her as you should so your prayers will not be hindered.
>
> 1 Peter 3:7

We live in a broken world where most people are not following God. We may have the opportunity to be agents of change, but it can be difficult when your spouse does not want to follow God. Some of the believers in the New Testament had unsaved spouses. Those believers wanted to go save the world. They wanted to abandon themselves to God's work, but their spouses would have nothing to do with it. When they asked Paul what to do, he gave this genius answer,

> If a fellow believer has a wife who is not a believer and she is willing to continue living with him, he must not leave her. And if a believing woman has a husband who is not a believer and he is willing to continue living with her, she must not leave him. For the believing wife brings holiness to her marriage, and the believing husband brings holiness to his marriage. Otherwise, your children would not be holy, but now they are holy. Don't you wives realize that your husbands might be saved because of you? And don't you husbands realize that your wives might be saved because of you?

> Each of you should continue to live in whatever situation the Lord has placed you, and remain as you were when God first called you.
>
> 1 Corinthians 7:12-17

In the same way that we do not need to abandon our old friends, we do not need to leave our unbelieving spouses. Our faith might be their salvation. The same Biblical advice works for young people. Young people are under the authority of their parents. Pushing back against that authority or expecting your parents to understand your new faith never works. Instead, you can follow God, respect your parents, and allow them to bless you because of your faith. Young people are given far more privileges when they live peacefully and respectfully with their parents. Perhaps God said it best in the Ten Commandments,

Honor your father and mother. Then you will live a long, full life in the land the Lord your God is giving you.

Exodus 20:12

Young people should listen to their parents instruction. And Christian parents long for their children to follow God. But pushing a child too much never works (see **Ephesians 6:4**). You need to remember that God is the one who draws your children.

Ephesians 6:4

Parents, do not provoke your children to anger by the way you treat them. Rather, bring them up with the discipline and instruction that comes from the Lord.

Peace and patience are the keys to living with an unbelieving family. You could be their salvation, but it is unlikely that they will choose God if you are pushy, offensive, and self-righteous.

6 How well do you live before your family? Are there any changes you should make so they can see God's love through your life?

_____

_____

_____

Live your faith because you love God. Live your faith because it is the right thing to do. And be patient with your friends and family. Your greatest hope with family members is to live your life so well that their arguments end up empty. When they finally accept the good change in you, they might become believers themselves.

7 Do you have family members who do not believe in God? If so, stop for a minute, write down their names, and say a prayer for them.

_____

_____

_____

HOW DO I ANSWER THE QUESTIONS?

Truth be told, most people will not oppose you. People hate conflict. But people will ask you questions as you continue to grow and succeed by living out God's commands. Your friends may ask, "What's changed in your life? You seem so different." New acquaintances might say, "You really seem to have it together. How do you do it?" Good living and prosperity get noticed, and those initial questions will most likely lead to other questions. People are interested in things that work. So how do you answer their questions?

Start by sharing your story. It is easy to share how your life is more peaceful because you are following God. It is easy to share how great forgiveness feels. It is easy to share your journey in everyday conversation. It is easy to say, "Yeah. I can't do that. I mean, I don't want to do that anymore. I like being sober."

But the more you change, and people see the changes, the more difficult the questions can become. The better you live, the more they will think you have all the answers. If they only knew! How do you answer questions that you have no idea how to answer? Be honest. Do not give cheesy answers or pretend that something unclear is clear. Be honest and say, "I have no idea how to explain it," or, "I really don't know, but I can try to find an answer."

The humility of honesty is compelling. God is so far beyond our understanding. There are things about our faith that we will struggle to comprehend. Sometimes, your only answer is to tell how God has changed your life. God did not call you to be a Bible scholar. He called you to be a follower. But, you do have access to all of his wisdom. You do have access to the Bible. Do you remember James's words about prayer?

> If you need wisdom, ask our generous God, and he will give it to you. He will not rebuke you for asking.
>
> James 1:5

Do you remember Paul's words to Timothy?

> You have been taught the holy Scriptures from childhood, and they have given you the wisdom to receive the salvation that comes by trusting in Christ Jesus. All Scripture is inspired by God and is useful to teach us what is true and to make us realize what is wrong in our lives. It corrects us when we are wrong and teaches us to do what is right. God uses it to prepare and equip his people to do every good work.
>
> 2 Timothy 3:15

You will never know everything about God, but you can know a lot. Maybe this is why Peter taught,

> And if someone asks about your hope as a believer, always be ready to explain it. But do this in a gentle and respectful way.
>
> 1 Peter 3:15-16

Humility and honesty go a long way when you cannot answer your friends' questions. But finding answers to their questions is an excellent opportunity for both of you. They get answers, and you learn more about God. So, search your Bible or get with a more experienced follower and find those answers. When you know the answer to a question, you can be strategic in how you answer. Did you know it is easier to teach someone something when they ask a question? It makes sense; people are prepared to listen when they ask a question. Authors, songwriters, and marketing pros leverage this principle as they prompt you to ask questions. Will the hero win? What is love like? Why do I need a new laundry detergent?

They are leveraging the power of storytelling. People want stories to end well. People want the plots of life to be resolved. And people will ask and ask until they get the answer. You can leverage the power of storytelling by controlling your excitement. Instead of opening the fire hydrant of your wisdom and passion, give people a trickle when they ask questions. Give them an appetizer instead of the whole enchilada. Let them think and ask the next question. Let them look for the coming resolution. You will be amazed at how much better you answer when you listen. Making your story a slow journey allows you to listen to God and figure out what they are really asking. Resist the temptation to tell people everything all at once. Do not overwhelm them. You can just give a short answer to their question and leave room for their next question.

Your new life will spill out in many ways. Your stories about the weekend will involve church. Your excitement and thankfulness about answered prayers will spill out at lunch. Your amazement at things you cannot comprehend will be seen. The new "why's" for your better decisions will be heard in the break room. People will be drawn to your hope and confidence. And, people will ask questions. You can worry about how you will answer, or you can embrace the powerful opportunity of answering.

8 List anyone who has recently shown an interest in your life. How did you respond?

_____

_____

_____

DO I FOLLOW GOD OR FOLLOW MY EARTHLY LEADERS?

Day 6

Paul taught that all earthly leaders are given to us by God for our good. (see Romans 13:1). Peter made the famous remark, "Fear God and respect the king!"

> For the Lord's sake, submit to all human authority—whether the king as head of state, or the officials he has appointed. For the king has sent them to punish those who do wrong and to honor those who do right. It is God's will that your honorable lives should silence those ignorant people who make foolish accusations against you. For you are free, yet you are God's slaves, so don't use your freedom as an excuse to do evil. Respect everyone, and love the family of believers. Fear God, and respect the king.
>
> 1 Peter 2:13-17

Romans 13:1

Everyone must submit to governing authorities. For all authority comes from God, and those in positions of authority have been placed there by God.

When the religious leaders tried to trap Jesus with a question about paying taxes, he said,

> ...give to Caesar what belongs to Caesar, and give to God what belongs to God."
>
> Matthew 22:21

Peter's words make the point. We can win favor and grace and show our leaders the power of God by living honorable lives that follow our leaders. Being an excellent employee is a powerful testimony of God's character. You can reach, sway, and even win over leaders by living godly as you work, serve, and follow them. Nehemiah was a captive of war. Fundamentally, he was a slave serving the new king. But as he served his king well and with honor, his long, steady service and prayers won over the king. Nehemiah's secular king ended up helping to rebuild Nehemiah's hometown of Jerusalem -- the very city from which Nehemiah became a prisoner of war (you can read the whole story in the Book of Nehemiah in the Old Testament).

Mordecai was also living in exile after Israel had been defeated by foreigners. He followed the rules until one of their leaders, Haman, demanded that Mordecai bow and worship him. Mordecai refused to worship anyone but God. So Haman set out to destroy Mordecai. God not only defended Mordecai, but God also gave Mordecai favor with Haman's boss. In the end, Haman got fired, and Mordecai became essential to the Jews finding a better life and favor in exile (read Esther in the Bible).

Another follower, Joseph, was sold into slavery to the Egyptian king. He served well and lived honorably, just like Nehemiah and Mordecai. His steady service and the evidence of his faith won over his leaders. The king eventually gave God credit and made Joseph his right-hand man (see Genesis 37, 39-41).

God is bigger than governments. Good always wins. Follow your bosses, governments, and authorities unless they force you to not follow God. But, even then, you should be willing to suffer the consequences with grace, peace, and respect.

Daniel lived out his faith, followed the laws of the land, and shared God's wisdom as a prisoner of war. When praying was outlawed in the nation, Daniel chose to keep praying, but that got him thrown to the lions. In an incredible miracle, the lions did not consume Daniel, and the power of God was displayed. The king made Daniel the nation's boss, and God got the glory.

Respectful, well-meaning believers have long demonstrated God's love, peace, and hope to their leaders. The list of heroes goes on and on. Some were delivered. Others died. But each made an impact as they lived faithful to God, following God and their earthly leaders.

It is unlikely that you will have to die for your faith, but you will undoubtedly have earthly leaders. Fear God and respect the king. Like many before you, your steady, excellent, faithful service can bring light to your leaders. You might even lead them to God as they lead you at work.

9 Are you living a godly, honorable, hard-working, good-following life with your earthly leaders? With your church leaders? How can you improve?

_____

_____

_____

10 Write this week's memory verse in the margin.

AT THE END OF THE WEEK ANSWER THESE QUESTIONS

What was the most meaningful statement(s) or scripture this week?	Reword the statement or scripture into a prayer of response to God.	What actions do you need to take in response to this week's study?

TRUTH 11

MEMORY VERSE

Work willingly at whatever you do, as though you were working for the Lord rather than for people.

Colossians 3:23

The Workplace

Who Do You Work For?

I was working for the second largest bank in the United States when Dan, the head of the Vehicle Sales and Finance Division, recruited me. He had noticed my ability to solve problems, and he had a handful. What Dan didn't know was that my problem-solving ability was fueled by my faith and God's methods for doing business. And that was a problem.

Dan and his gang of retail and fleet vehicle financiers were old-school car sales guys. They were smoke encrusted with hair slicked back, wearing fine suits as they retired to the stripper bars at lunch. It was something out of a movie. Needless to say, I didn't fit in. I began working on Dan's problems and quickly discovered the rumors of classic used car sales tactics were true. I found falsified credit, debt, and collection reports. Sales reports weren't any better. It was a real smoke and mirrors operation. As instructed, I began to design and implement solutions. I forwarded the corrected reports to management. I highlighted credit policies that needed to be changed. I challenged his team about their profit claims on fleet sales. I uncovered kickbacks. What did Dan do? Nothing. He did not forward the correct reports or make the changes. He did not fire his gang of conspirators. Nothing changed, and that was a problem for me.

Time after time, I went to Dan, asking him what he was going to do about all these crimes. Time after time, I warned him that he would get in trouble. The bank was being ripped off. The customers were being ripped off. The federal regulators were hot on the trail. But Dan did nothing.

I remember the day that Dan and his accomplices finally threatened me. "If you tell anyone, you will never work in banking. Never! We know people. You work for us, and you don't want to go against us! Do you understand?" My only response was that I worked for the company. The CEO signed my checks. "We will ruin you!" they threatened again. It was then that I took a stand and said, "You know guys, God got me this job. His principles have made me successful. If you can fire me, then fire me. But as long as I am here, I am going to do things right and trust God to keep making me successful." Boy, you should have seen their faces!

Long story short, two of them ended up in jail. The rest went back to their used car lots. I ended up working for the board of directors. Good always wins when you remember that you are working for God, follow his ways, and do great, honest work.

QUICK, SMART START

A WORKING ATTITUDE

It can be challenging to live your new life at work. Your coworkers knew the old you pretty well. They saw your rough edges. They laughed alongside you at jokes that now leave you feeling uneasy. Your coworkers heard you criticize bad bosses and slower peers. They may have seen you skim a deal or take a sick day when you were not ill. But even if your character was good before Christ, there is no doubt that they are noticing a difference in you.

Colossians 3:23

Work willingly at whatever you do, as though you were working for the Lord rather than for people.

Once people find out that you are a Christian, they will hold you to a higher standard. Some may try to disprove God by proving that you have not changed. If your good life convicts coworkers, they might push back or persecute you. But there is opportunity and power in work-life. God's principles for business are practical. You can excel at work by applying His wisdom. Your sales can go up. Your administrative work can serve the staff better than ever before. Your attitude can lift the altitude of the office. You can show people the value of following God as you follow God at work.

We spend about one-third of our life and half of our waking hours at work. It is no wonder that God teaches us so much about how to work. He tells us to work hard, well, with integrity, and so much more. His truths about prayer, the Holy Spirit, knowing His will, making choices, materialism, and sin apply as we live at work. You become a powerhouse at work when you combine His work truths with the other truths you have learned.

Your time at work is not just working; it is half of your life. And work is purposeful to God. It began in the garden when Adam and Eve tended to the garden. He designed us to work and created us to enjoy being productive at work.

> The Lord God placed the man in the Garden of Eden to tend and watch over it.
>
> Genesis 2:15

From the beginning, God designed us to work. There is fulfillment in work. There is incredible value in doing our work well and creating good things. The first place of worship was built to exact specifications. It was constructed beautifully. God's principles of working the farm are detailed. When farmers follow those principles, they get bountiful crops. Honesty in our work is commended by God. Integrity in our work is commanded by God. God sees our work as being done for him, even when we do it for others.

> In all the work you are doing, work the best you can. Work as if you were doing it for the Lord, not for people.
>
> Colossians 3:23 NCV

What we build, make, and do should be done as if it were a work we were presenting to God himself. From his perspective, that is precisely what we are doing.

What we build, make, and do should be done as if it were a work we were presenting to God himself. From his perspective, that is precisely what we are doing. If you ever wondered what God wanted you to do, you can be sure he wants you to work and work well. But God's design was larger than the work in the garden.

 Read the following verse. List the things God wanted Adam and Eve to do beyond working in the garden.

> So God created human beings. In the image of God he created them; male and female he created them. Then God blessed them and said, "Be fruitful and multiply. Fill the earth and govern it. Reign over the fish in the sea, the birds in the sky, and all the animals that scurry along the ground."
>
> Genesis 1:27-28

_____

_____

God wanted Adam and Eve to expand their world. They were the beginning of humankind, and he wanted them to fill the entire earth. They were the caretakers and managers of humanity and all creation. That role has not changed. Biblical scholars refer to Genesis 1:27-28 as the "cultural mandate." Bob Thune explained it this way in his article "Created for Work",

> God is mandating that humans will create culture. Adam and Eve will produce children. Those children will create families, and those families will band together into cities and social networks.

Those networks of human beings will reflect all the aspects of human culture—language and art and music and food and philosophy and theology.

Work is part of a healthy life, and working well should be the goal of every disciple. But God wants even more for you at work. You not only have the opportunity to produce good products, technology, and service, you have the opportunity to bring a better life to the people at work. You can build a culture. You have the opportunity to advance God's love, truth, and principles as you advance in your work. Your work and how you work can be quiet, persuasive examples of God's goodness. You can change the culture of your workplace as you follow and then one day as you lead.

❷ Write and practice this week's memory verse.

_____

_____

_____

HOW SHOULD I FOLLOW MY BOSSES?

Your bosses are your bosses. Your company pays you. You should respect their position and be thankful for their guidance and provision. Paul taught that our authorities, even the ones that need improvement, are given by God and can be used for our good.

❸ Read the verses below and write the truths about your bosses and authorities at work in the following blanks.

¹Everyone must submit to governing authorities. For all authority comes from God, and those in positions of authority have been placed there by God. ²So anyone who rebels against authority is rebelling against what God has instituted, and they will be punished. ³For the authorities do not strike fear in people who are doing right, but in those who are doing wrong. Would you

like to live without fear of the authorities? Do what is right, and they will honor you. ⁴The authorities are God's servants, sent for your good. But if you are doing wrong, of course you should be afraid, for they have the power to punish you. They are God's servants, sent for the very purpose of punishing those who do what is wrong. ⁵So you must submit to them, not only to avoid punishment, but also to keep a clear conscience.

Romans 13:1-5

- verse 1 _____

- verse 2 _____

- verse 3 _____

- verse 4 _____

- verse 5 _____

All authority comes from God. God is aware that your boss is your boss. From God's perspective, he knowingly made your boss your boss when he led you to take the job (verse 1). Because God made your boss your boss, if you rebel against your boss, you are actually rebelling against God's plan (verse 2). Work well if you do not want to fear your boss (verse 3). God gave you your boss to hold you accountable for good work (verse 4). God actually sees them as his servants for your good. But the most significant reason to follow and respect your boss is to have a clear conscience (verse 5).

Doing our work well wins in the end. Even unrighteous supervisors reward good work. You may work for an unfair boss, but you still need to work as if you are working for God.

> Obey your earthly masters in everything you do. Try to please them all the time, not just when they are watching you. Serve them sincerely because of your reverent fear of the Lord. Work willingly at whatever you do, as though you were working for the Lord rather than for people. 24Remember that the Lord will give you an inheritance as your reward, and that the Master you are serving is Christ.
>
> Colossians 3:22-24

Trust God to deal with your bosses. Allow him to reward you for your good work. Your bosses are accountable to God for their good or bad leadership. You should follow them unless following them causes you to not obey God. You should serve your supervisors and company as if Jesus were your employer.

❹ Take a moment and write a prayer for your boss. A prayer for his success, spiritual life, and his family.

_____

_____

_____

Have you ever felt like a slave at work? Slavery existed in the New Testament times. It was not right, but it was reality. Slaves could not just stop being slaves. As slaves became Christians, Paul taught them to live in their current situation. Paul encouraged these new believers to go far beyond being slaves. He encouraged them to see themselves as a testimony.

> Slaves should yield to their own masters at all times, trying to please them and not arguing with them. They should not steal from them but should show their masters they can be fully trusted so that in everything they do they will make the teaching of God our Savior attractive.
>
> Titus 2:9-10

Paul's teaching to those who became believers while in slavery is reminiscent of Joseph's life in the Old Testament. Joseph was sold into slavery, but he followed God. He gained wisdom from God and served so well that his master made him the boss of everything in Egypt. Again, we see the principle that good always wins. Good wins even when good has to show itself under oppression. You may not live under slavery, but there are times when you cannot quit a lousy job. There are times when you have to work under a slave driver of a boss. In these moments of life, embrace Paul's teaching and go far beyond your boss's expectations. Use your excellent character to make our God attractive. Paul taught the Ephesian this about working,

> Obey your earthly masters with deep respect and fear. Serve them sincerely as you would serve Christ. Try to please them all the time, not just when they are watching you. As slaves of Christ, do the will of God with all your heart. Work with enthusiasm, as though you were working for the Lord rather than for people. Remember that the Lord will reward each one of us for the good we do, whether we are slaves or free.
>
> Ephesians 6:5-8

Whether you have a good boss or a bad boss, submitting to his authority is what God wants. Listening to and respecting your boss may allow you to offer new ideas and evoke positive change. Excellent work provides your greatest opportunity to improve your work life and your workplace's culture.

 Is your boss a good boss or a bad boss? What can you do to improve your relationship with your boss or further support him?

_____

_____

Here are a few more tips on supervisor and company relations adapted from "The Christian at Work", a bible study by Craig Ledbetter.

- Respect your company's property. It does not belong to you (see **Leviticus 19:11**).
- Do a fair day's work for your pay. Laziness is a form of theft (see **Proverbs 18:9**, Proverbs 14:23).
- Help your company succeed and make your employer look good (see Genesis 31:39-45).
- Mind your own business and do not let others affect your work (see **2 Thessalonians 3:11-12**).

Leviticus 19:11
Do not steal. Do not deceive or cheat one another.

Proverbs 18:9
A lazy person is as bad as someone who destroys things.

2 Thessalonians 3:11-12
Yet we hear that some of you are living idle lives, refusing to work and meddling in other people's business. We command such people and urge them in the name of the Lord Jesus Christ to settle down and work to earn their own living.

- Work for the wage you negotiated. Do not compare salaries. If you want to make more, do great work, then renegotiate (Matthew 20:1-16).

6 Looking at the list above, are there any improvements you need to make in the workplace?

_____

_____

_____

HOW SHOULD I TREAT MY EMPLOYEES?

If you follow well, it is likely that you will eventually lead others. And leading can be challenging. You have quotas, goals, and responsibilities. Things need to get done, and your workers need to get them done. While trying to balance everything, it is easy to become the "bad boss."

In his book "Good Boss, Bad Boss," Robert Sutton says that the last one to know he is a bad boss is the boss himself. Great leaders combat this tendency with self-awareness. They use self-awareness to hone and improve their leadership skills. They ask themselves tough questions to develop empathy and grace towards their employees. Here are a few questions to check your leadership against Biblical teaching.

Do you pay them a fair wage?

For the Scripture says, ... "The laborer is worthy of his wages."
1 Timothy 5:18 HCSB

Never take advantage of poor and destitute laborers, whether they are fellow Israelites or foreigners living in your towns. You must pay them their wages each day before sunset because they are poor and are counting on it. If you don't, they might cry out to the Lord against you, and it would be counted against you as sin.
Deuteronomy 24:14-15

You should always pay a fair wage. Never cheat a worker to increase your profits. You are God's instrument to provide for your workers' needs as they provide for your success. You need to pay them well and on time.

Are you looking out for their best interests?

> If then there is any encouragement in Christ, if any consolation of love, if any fellowship with the Spirit, if any affection and mercy, fulfill my joy by thinking the same way, having the same love, sharing the same feelings, focusing on one goal. Do nothing out of rivalry or conceit, but in humility consider others as more important than yourselves. Everyone should look out not only for his own interests, but also for the interests of others.
>
> Philippians 2:1-4 HCSB

You are God's instrument to provide for your workers' needs as they provide for your success. You need to pay them well and on time.

Your employees are God's creation. You are merely a steward of His workers. You should be a gift to your workers in the same way your authorities are supposed to be God's gift for your good. Always look out for your employees' best interests.

Are you raising your workers up to be future leaders?

> Now these are the gifts Christ gave to the church: the apostles, the prophets, the evangelists, and the pastors and teachers. Their responsibility is to equip God's people to do his work and build up the church, the body of Christ.
>
> Ephesians 4:11-12

God has given us spiritual leaders to equip us. They are responsible for building us up, training us, and preparing us to do the works of God. In the same way, you should be equipping your physical workers to be the next generation of leaders in your workplace. You should be helping each worker become a better worker. Helping others improve is the greatest privilege of leadership.

Are you being a good boss?

> Masters, in the same way, be good to your slaves. Do not threaten them. Remember that the One who is your Master and their Master is in heaven, and he treats everyone alike.
>
> Ephesians 6:9

This verse addressed those who had slaves or servants, but it applies even more to you and your employees. The best boss is a consistently good boss. God is the only true master. He is the ultimate employer. You should be good to your employees. You should be kind and gracious, even while pushing them to improve.

Do you have the heart and mind of a servant?

Matthew 7:12

Do to others whatever you would like them to do to you. This is the essence of all that is taught in the law and the prophets.

Jesus called them together and said, "The other nations have rulers. You know that those rulers love to show their power over the people, and their important leaders love to use all their authority. But it should not be that way among you. Whoever wants to become great among you must serve the rest of you like a servant. Whoever wants to become the first among you must serve all of you like a slave. In the same way, the Son of Man did not come to be served. He came to serve others and to give his life as a ransom for many people."

Mark 10:42-45 NCV

Jesus is the King of the Universe, but when he lived on earth, he served those around him. Leaders have the privilege of serving those that they lead. Service is the pinnacle of maturity for you as a boss.

Always treat your employees the way you want to be treated. (see Matthew 7:12) Always seek their best. Invest in your workers. Pay them fairly and timely. Share the success with your workers. Lead as if you are Christ.

 Rate your leadership in the following areas using a scale of 1 to 5, with 5 being the best. Circle your answer.

1 2 3 4 5   I pay my workers a fair wage.

1 2 3 4 5   I look out for their best interests.

1 2 3 4 5   I raise my workers up to be future leaders.

1 2 3 4 5   I am a good boss.

1 2 3 4 5   I have the heart and mind of a servant

8 How can you improve your boss skills?

_____

_____

_____

_____

HOW SHOULD I TREAT MY CUSTOMERS?

Customers are not just part of your work. Customers are the work. No matter what your company creates, provides, or champions, your success is entirely based on customers buying it. You might be six steps behind direct customer interaction, but your work still impacts your customers. The quality and quantity of your work affect future sales and corporate growth. Even behind the scenes, you should do your work with customer satisfaction in mind.

And when you come into contact with your customers, you should treat them fairly. They should see your godly character in action. Beyond being your customers, they are people. They are God's creation. You should treat them with respect. Each of us reaps what we sow. Peace begets peace, and stress generates stress. Even with grumpy customers, a wise answer always wins. Solomon put it this way,

> A gentle answer deflects anger, but harsh words make tempers flare.
>
> Proverbs 15:1

Respecting your customers also means dealing with them fairly. The Israelites were primarily an agricultural society using scales to measure products and conduct trade. Again and again, God told them to be fair.

> The Lord hates dishonest scales, but he is pleased with honest weights.
>
> Proverbs 11:1 NCV

> Do not cheat when you measure the length or weight, or amount of something. Your weights and balances should weigh correctly, with your weighing baskets the right size and your jars holding the right amount of liquid.
>
> Leviticus 19:35-36

Some salespeople inflate the value of their products. Some salespeople use fear as a sales motivator. Other salespeople stretch the truth to make a deal. Lying and being dishonest to your customers may increase your profits or close a sale, but it will steal your soul.

> Better to be poor and honest than to be dishonest and rich.
>
> Proverbs 28:6

You never ever want your business dealings to derail your faith. Profit is not worth your soul. Jesus said it best,

> And what do you benefit if you gain the whole world but lose your own soul? Is anything worth more than your soul?
>
> Matthew 16:26

Your role in customer service allows you to serve your customers and build mutual respect. Honesty, excellent service, and a fair price should be your standard of good work.

You will spend a third of your life following God at work. You can pray and leverage God's truths for success. You can lead and raise up employees and peers using God's truths. You can seek His wisdom when evaluating business deals and solving problems. You can capitalize on the strength of the Holy Spirit when you are beyond your limits. Excellent work brings influence. Influence opens the doors to promotions, leadership, and sharing the source of your success.

Excellent work brings influence. Influence opens the doors to promotions, leadership, and sharing the source of your success.

❾ Are you aware of any of your business dealings or work that could compromise your integrity, the quality of your product, or your company's reputation? If so, what will you do to change?

_____

_____

_____

10 Write and practice this week's memory verse.

_____

_____

_____

AT THE END OF THE WEEK ANSWER THESE QUESTIONS

What was the most meaningful statement(s) or scripture this week?	Reword the statement or scripture into a prayer of response to God.	What actions do you need to take in response to this week's study?

TRUTH 12

MEMORY VERSE

You must each decide in your heart how much to give. And don't give reluctantly or in response to pressure. "For God loves a person who gives cheerfully."

2 Corinthians 9:7

Tithes and Offerings

Money, Money, Money

I am a bit dazed and confused when it comes to Christians talking about giving money to God. A wealthy acquaintance once said, "If I give ten percent, I would be giving $100,000. That is like ten percent of the church budget. I give less so others will have to do their part." A controlling acquaintance said, "I designate my giving because the church should give more to missions." A selfish acquaintance said, "I don't have to give. I am free in Christ," but of course, he enjoyed the programs, ate the food, and used the toilet paper. A giving acquaintance said, "I already give ten percent. That is what God said to give. I am not giving any more than that." And the sayings go on.

Churches aren't much better at talking about giving. Some are legalistic and teach giving ten percent of your earnings to God. Others agree but disagree about giving ten percent of your gross or net pay. Some, seeking balance, say, "Ten percent is the number God gave in his laws to the Israelites. Why would we do any less?" Some get the heart of the matter and stress that we should give thankfully and willingly. Others, wanting to feel free, focus on Paul's teaching that we get to decide how much to give. They say, "After all, aren't Christians free from the Old Law?"

I found freedom when Joe Durham said to me, "Doug. Grace always outperforms the law. So when it comes to money, grace always ends up giving more. Not because it has to but because it chooses to." Joe told me that people full of the Holy Spirit, those who feel the grace of forgiveness, are generous givers. They would invest anything for people to find what they found. They aren't materialistic. People who understand how graceful God is are filled with generosity. They are not trying to do less; they are trying to do more.

Joe believed all of this, trusted God in me, and I figured it out. Being generous has been my privilege, and I am thankful to those who taught me God's truths. Giving back to God is required. Giving back to God is fun. Being an outrageous giver has never left me wanting. I can give more than ten percent because I have all I need. Giving to those in need is God providing through me for them. Giving to God spreads the Good News about Jesus. Giving allows me to be involved in what God is doing. I cannot out give God. I love giving. I hope you find the joy in thanking God and helping others through giving.

GIVING TO GOD

Genesis 4:3-4

When it was time for the harvest, Cain presented some of his crops as a gift to the Lord. Abel also brought a gift—the best portions of the firstborn lambs from his flock.

Hebrews 7:4

Consider then how great this Melchizedek was. Even Abraham, the great patriarch of Israel, recognized this by giving him a tenth of what he had taken in battle.

Genesis 28:22

I will present to God a tenth of everything he gives me.

Believers have a long history of giving to God. Adam and Eve were the first people. Their two sons, Cain and Abel, made offerings to God from their growing crops and flocks (see Genesis 4:3-4). We presume that the boys learned this practice from their parents, who learned it from God. Abraham gave a tenth of the plunder after God helped him win a battle (see Genesis 14:19-20, Hebrews 7:4). Abraham's grandson, Jacob, promised to give a tenth of all God gave him (see Genesis 28:13-22). When God established his followers as a nation, God made giving a law for the Israelites (see Leviticus 27:30-32, Deuteronomy 14:22). In his day, Jesus affirmed the Jewish leaders for giving a tenth of all they gained even though he questioned their motives (see Matthew 23:23). Jesus even taught about giving more than a tenth as he commended a poor widow for giving her all (see Mark 12:41-44).

These believers were not just giving; they were giving back to God. Their attitude was one of gratefulness and gratitude. They believed in God and knew that everything they gained, everything they had, was given by God. They were thanking God for providing. They acknowledged that He was the one who blessed them with an increase.

God's word for returning ten percent to him is "tithing." Giving a tithe is returning ten percent of all your increase to God. And these believers gave from the first fruits. They gave off their gross increase, not their net profit.

> Honor the Lord with your wealth and with the first fruits of all your produce; then your barns will be filled with plenty, and your vats will be bursting with wine.
>
> Proverbs 3:9-10

Regardless of their expenses, they gave a tenth of the total crop, a tenth of the total new animals, and a tenth of their total gain back to God (see Deuteronomy 26:2).

> One-tenth of the produce of the land, whether grain from the fields or fruit from the trees, belongs to the Lord and must be set apart to him as holy.
>
> Leviticus 27:30

TITHES AND OFFERINGS

❶ Do you give a tithe, ten percent of all you earn, back to God? Why or why not?

_____

_____

_____

Believers also gave God other gifts called sacrifices and offerings. Some sacrifices and offerings were made in recognition of sin and guilt. These sacrifices were voluntary, each representing a desire for forgiveness. Christians do not make these sacrifices because Jesus forgave all sin with one sacrifice -- his life.

Other offerings were thankful offerings for good harvests, bountiful herds, and increased profits. These offerings were voluntary gifts to God. There is no Biblical record of believers practicing these types of voluntary offerings after Jesus paid the price of sin and rose to give all believers new life.

From the beginning of humanity, those that believe in God have given back to God. They gave out of thankfulness, recognizing God as their provider. They listened to his words and his commands. They feared, or better, respected God. Giving back to him was acknowledging Him as God, their provider. Giving back to him was worship. Giving back to God was their statement that all they had was God's.

Even after Jesus went to heaven, believers continued to give to God and others. Christians gave a portion of their grain and gain to his Church. They gave portions of their grain and gain to support God's workers. They gave portions of their grain and gain to help those in need. And, the believers who received the Holy Spirit of God after Jesus ascended to heaven gave far more than a tenth.

❷ How many dollars do you give in your tithe? How many dollars do you regularly give beyond your tithe? How many dollars do you give to special offerings or needs?

_____

_____

Leviticus 27:30-32

One-tenth of the produce of the land, whether grain from the fields or fruit from the trees, belongs to the Lord and must be set apart to him as holy. Count off every tenth animal from your herds and flocks and set them apart for the Lord as holy.

Mark 12:43-44

I tell you the truth, this poor widow has given more than all the others who are making contributions. For they gave a tiny part of their surplus, but she, poor as she is, has given everything she had to live on.

QUICK, SMART START

③ Write and practice this week's memory verse.

_____

_____

_____

TITHES AND OFFERINGS TODAY

The topic of giving was easy for the Israelites. They had direct instructions from God. God told them when, why, and how much to give. God told them to bring offerings to build His place of worship (see Exodus 25:1-9). He told them to bring special offerings when they were thankful and when they were repenting. He told them to bring offerings to help orphans, widows, the poor, and the needy (see Deuteronomy 15:7-11). And God told them what to bring.

He also told them to give a tenth of their increase, whether it be animals, crops, or financial increase. A tenth of everything was to be given back to God. And he was serious about this instruction. He told the Israelites that they were robbing God when they did not tithe.

> You have cheated me of the tithes and offerings due to me. You are under a curse, for your whole nation has been cheating me. Bring all the tithes into the storehouse so there will be enough food in my Temple. If you do," says the Lord of Heaven's Armies, "I will open the windows of heaven for you. I will pour out a blessing so great you won't have enough room to take it in! Try it! Put me to the test! Your crops will be abundant, for I will guard them from insects and disease. Your grapes will not fall from the vine before they are ripe," says the Lord of Heaven's Armies. "Then all nations will call you blessed, for your land will be such a delight," says the Lord of Heaven's Armies.
>
> Malachi 3:7-12

The principles of giving were easy to understand. God explained his principles and gave the Israelites instruction. He even disciplined and rewarded his children as they applied his truths of giving. God wanted his people to remember that he was the provider of all things. He wanted them to remember that with him, they would never want for anything. God did not need their money, crops, and animals. They needed to remember Him, be free from materialism, and trust Him to provide. God's commandments are always for our benefit, not his.

God also told them how to use the tithes and offerings. The tithe was to support the priests. Some offerings helped maintain the place where the Israelites worshipped. Some offerings were used to support the needy. The instructions were clear. The Israelites knew how to honor God and follow him regarding giving.

Some Christians question whether they should tithe because the New Testament does not teach much about tithing. How silly! The New Testament does not say much about murder, but no one wonders if we should murder. The New Testament says nothing about cannibalism, but no one wonders if we should eat people. Christians are not bound by the law. We are not judged acceptable or unacceptable to God based on how we follow God's commands. Christians are accepted by God because of Jesus' sacrifice and his unconditional love. But the wisdom and principles of God found in the Law still apply. The New Testament always inherits the wisdom of the Old Testament.

4 The most comprehensive record of God's desire for his followers to give back to him is found in the laws he established for his nation Israel. Do you believe God's desires have changed?

_____

_____

5 Have you ever cheated God by not seeing the tithe as holy and set apart for him?

_____

_____

QUICK, SMART START

Tithing and giving are Biblical concepts. Believers knew to give tithes and offerings long before God wrote down his instructions. They knew that everything good came from God. There was a reason that Abraham tithed. There were reasons that God instructed the Israelites to give. And there is a reason that God takes tithing so seriously that he disciplines those who do not tithe. Some of those reasons were spiritual. Some of those reasons were practical. But all the reasons to give continue to this day.

Day 3: WHY SHOULD I TITHE AND GIVE OFFERINGS?

All of your income and increase are God's. God gives you one hundred percent of all that you get.

> Beware lest you say in your heart, 'My power and the might of my hand have gotten me this wealth.' You shall remember the Lord your God, for it is he who gives you power to get wealth,
>
> Deuteronomy 8:17-18 ESV

You should tithe because the first tenth of all your increase is God's. In fact, God sees this tenth as holy, set apart for him and his alone.

> One-tenth of the produce of the land, whether grain from the fields or fruit from the trees, belongs to the Lord and must be set apart to him as holy.
>
> Leviticus 27:30

He instructs you to return ten percent to Him. And, he wants you to manage the other ninety percent according to his principles.

The tithe has two purposes. First, when you tithe, you recognize that everything is God's and that all your increase is God's. He is the Lord. He is the Creator. He is the Provider. Every time you tithe, you exhibit faith. Every time you tithe, you reaffirm what you said when you first believed: God is God. You are saying, "Thank you for your glorious creation. Thank you for creating me to work and allowing me to prosper this week. Thank you for providing. All I have is yours."

Second, God is helping you fight materialism and teaching you to live by faith. It is challenging to give away ten percent of your income. If you spend what you make, you might think, "I have no money left over. How can I take a 10% pay cut? How will I pay the bills?" If you are good at saving, you tend to keep saving. You see your savings as a necessary expense. In both cases, it takes faith and change to follow God and give back a tenth of your income. Do you believe in God's promises? Do you believe what he said to the Israelites when he told them to test him by giving? Do you believe He will provide you what you need and even more if you are faithful to give back to Him (see **Luke 6:38**)?

Tithing causes us to live our faith. It is one thing to say, "God provides everything." It is another to actually live out that statement. It takes faith and sacrifice to adjust your budget, cut out fun spending and allow for the tithe. It takes commitment to believe that the tenth is God's. Tithing goes against every materialistic bone in our bodies as it leads us to make all that we have available to God. Simply put, tithing requires faith.

6 Write a prayer to God asking him to help you be faithful and have the faith to give generously to him and his people.

_____

_____

_____

People who faithfully tithe will tell you of unexpected miracles and blessings. I have never met a person who tithes for the right reason and does not have all he needs. In fact, every faithful tither I have met has enough to share. God blesses those who are faithful with little, and he gives them more than they need. He can trust them to use his resources to not only meet their needs but to meet the needs of others.

God told the Israelites to tithe and told them the tithe should support those who worked in the temple. Paul reiterated this truth for Christians in the New Testament.

> Don't you realize that those who work in the temple get their meals from the offerings brought to the temple? And those who serve at the altar get a share of the sacrificial offerings. In the same way, the Lord ordered that those who preach the Good News should be supported by those who benefit from it.
> 1 Corinthians 9:13-14

Luke 6:38 ESV

Give, and it will be given to you. Good measure, pressed down, shaken together, running over, will be put into your lap. For with the measure you use it will be measured back to you.

> Those who are taught the word of God should provide for their teachers, sharing all good things with them.
>
> Galatians 6:6

Tithing provides for those that work for God. But there is so much more to giving than tithing. God required much more than ten percent in the Old Testament. If you add up their tithes and offerings, the Israelites gave roughly one-third of all they made. In the New Testament, Jesus and the apostles called us to an even higher standard. Jesus taught,

> Don't store treasures for yourselves here on earth where moths and rust will destroy them and thieves can break in and steal them. But store your treasures in heaven where they cannot be destroyed by moths or rust and where thieves cannot break in and steal them. Your heart will be where your treasure is.
>
> Matthew 6:19-21 NCV

If your heart is for God, you will invest in God, in God's work, and in God's people. The first tenth will go directly to God. The rest will be available to God and His people. Life is not money, but money can bring life to those in need. Money can bring the Good News to new places. When our heart is for God's work, our money will find its way there too. The love of God in us and our love for God should spur us to outrageous generosity. John taught,

> But whoever has the world's goods, and sees his brother in need and closes his heart against him, how does the love of God abide in him?
>
> 1 John 3:17

The inverse is true as well. If the love of God is alive in you, no one will have to tell you to give. You will gladly give the tithe and then give more to everyone in need. Trust God. You will never out give God if you give when He directs you to give. He will invest in you as you invest in His good works.

7 Do you see giving as a privilege of using God's resources to bless others? Why or why not?

_____

_____

_____

Giving has practical purposes, but there is a higher spiritual purpose to giving. Giving is good for us. Paul encouraged people to give, not for him, but for their own good.

> Really, it is not that I want to receive gifts from you, but I want you to have the good that comes from giving.
>
> Philippians 4:17 NCV

His words remind us of Jesus' words,

> I showed you in all things that you should work as I did and help the weak. I taught you to remember the words Jesus said: 'It is more blessed to give than to receive.'
>
> Acts 20:35 NCV

Giving the tithe, offerings beyond the tithe, and helping others in need are good for us. But where do you give those gifts? Who do you give your tithe to? Where do you invest your resources?

WHO DO I GIVE MY TITHES, OFFERINGS, AND GIFTS TO?

Day 4

The primary place where you give should be your church. Christians should provide well for their spiritual leaders. Christians should support the ministries of their local church.

The Israelites brought their tithes, offerings, and other gifts to the temple. The temple was the center of their faith community. The first Christians continued to worship God at the Jewish temple (see Acts 2:46) and gave their tithe there. As Christianity grew, the local church became the center of their faith community. And Christians brought their tithes to their local church. The New Testament model used the tithes to support the leaders and spread the Gospel.

The New Testament also records special offerings beyond the tithes. Luke, a Christian historian, wrote about an offering from all the churches to support the needs of the Jerusalem church.

During this time some prophets traveled from Jerusalem to Antioch. One of them named Agabus stood up in one of the meetings and predicted by the Spirit that a great famine was coming upon the entire Roman world. (This was fulfilled during the reign of Claudius.) So the believers in Antioch decided to send relief to the brothers and sisters in Judea, everyone giving as much as they could. This they did, entrusting their gifts to Barnabas and Saul to take to the elders of the church in Jerusalem.

Acts 11:27-30

Matthew 19:21

If you want to be perfect, go and sell all your possessions and give the money to the poor, and you will have treasure in heaven. Then come, follow me.

Again and again, we see Christians giving cheerful, willing gifts beyond their tithes. They even sold their property and assets to meet the church's and others' needs.

And all the believers met together in one place and shared everything they had. They sold their property and possessions and shared the money with those in need.

Acts 2:44-45

Leaders like Paul, who traveled to share the Gospel and start churches, were supported by individual Christians and churches. Paul wrote,

Even so, you have done well to share with me in my present difficulty. As you know, you Philippians were the only ones who gave me financial help when I first brought you the Good News and then traveled on from Macedonia. No other church did this. Even when I was in Thessalonica you sent help more than once.

Philippians 4:14-16

Luke 14:33

So you cannot become my disciple without giving up everything you own.

Jesus sent the first missionaries out, telling them to take no money but rely on those who received them to support them.

Stay in one place, eating and drinking what they provide. Don't hesitate to accept hospitality, because those who work deserve their pay.

Luke 10:7

So, where do you give? Give your tithe to your church. Give to the special offerings of your church according to your ability. If God leads you and you have the ability to give, give offerings and gifts directly to other ministries and individuals in need.

8 Where are you giving your tithe? Who are you giving your tithe to?

_____

_____

_____

HOW MUCH SHOULD I GIVE?

Day 5

How much should you give? The smallest amount God told us to give was ten percent of our gross income -- the tithe. The greatest amount was "Give everything!" (see **Matthew 19:21, Luke 14:33**). The amount you should give will most likely fall between those two answers.

After you adjust your budget and lifestyle to give the tithe, you should give as you have the capability. When it came to the offerings beyond the tithe, God told the Israelites,

> All must give as they are able, according to the blessings given to them by the Lord your God.
>
> Deuteronomy 16:16-17

Paul reiterated God's principle when he urged others to give a special offering to help believers during a famine. He wrote,

> Now concerning the money collected for the relief of the saints in Jerusalem, you are to do the same as I directed the churches of Galatia to do. On the first day of every week each one of you is to put something aside, in proportion to his prosperity, and save it so that no collections will need to be made when I come.
>
> 1 Corinthians 16:1-2

As you tithe and live responsibly, make outrageous giving your goal. Give in proportion to your blessing. Give far more than the tithe. Give out of the love of your heart. Enjoy giving.

QUICK, SMART START

❾ Read 2 Corinthians 9:7-8 and answer the questions below.

2 Corinthians 9:7-8

You must each decide in your heart how much to give. And don't give reluctantly or in response to pressure. "For God loves a person who gives cheerfully." And God will generously provide all you need. Then you will always have everything you need and plenty left over to share with others.

- Who determines the amount of your special offerings?

  _____

- What should your attitude be?

  _____

- What is God's promise to those that give generously?

  _____

In your heart, through prayer, you decide how much to give to special offerings. Giving should be fun and cheerful. You should give in proportion to the blessings of God. And God promises that you can never out-give his supply. God says that if you give, he will provide all you need.

Giving special offerings to your church and others takes a bit of balance. You need to be responsible, but you also need to have faith. God tells us to pay our bills. (see Romans 13:7-8). He tells us to take care of our families (see 1 Timothy 5:8). He tells us to pay our workers. (see Leviticus 19:13). But there are times when God leads us to risky giving that requires faith and sacrifice. God led the Christians in Macedonia to do just that. Paul tells us about their giving,

> I can tell you that they gave as much as they were able and even more than they could afford. No one told them to do it. But they begged and pleaded with us to let them share in this service for God's people. And they gave in a way we did not expect: They first gave themselves to the Lord and to us. This is what God wants.
>
> 2 Corinthians 8:3-5 NCV

In those risky offerings, we must embrace God's promise in Proverbs.

> One person gives freely, yet gains even more; another withholds unduly, but comes to poverty. A generous person will prosper; whoever refreshes others will be refreshed.
>
> Proverbs 11:24-25

Giving in the New Testament goes much further than a simple tithe. Giving is turning over complete control of your life and resources to Jesus Christ. If God has control of your life, He will have control of your resources. Your bank account is full of God's money. It should always be available to him. Your budget manages God's capital. It should allow you to tithe, give, and help others.

Ten percent of all your revenue is the lower limit to what you should give. The tithe is for your faith and good. There is no upper limit to what you can give. Fund as much of God's work to save the world as possible. Trust him to prosper you even more. Live responsibly and give outrageously.

WHAT IF I QUESTION HOW THE CHURCH IS USING THE MONEY?

Day 6

In most churches, the leaders are entrusted to handle the finances. If your church follows God's financial principles, you must trust your leaders.

You should ask if you have questions about how or in what the church is investing God's resources. Always assume the best. Assume that your leaders have prayed. Assume they have Biblical truths underlying their decisions. If you realize that the church is violating God's principles, you need to speak to the leaders. You need to work with the leaders, not against them. You must do your best to help your church stay united and follow God's principles.

But, in all of this, you must remain surrendered to God's principles. You should never withhold your tithe from God. You should never try to control the use of your tithe; even if you are trying to correct an error by your leaders. The tithe is not yours to manage. The tithe is God's, and the people that manage it are responsible for how they use his money. If they do not use the tithe properly, they are accountable to God. If you do not tithe, you are accountable to God. When a church does not use the tithe responsibly, there is a much bigger problem. You might need to change churches. But you should never withhold your tithe from God. You are giving it to him, not them.

QUICK, SMART START

The most crucial principle of tithing is surrendering what is God's back to God. If your church misses this truth, if they misuse the tithes for frivolous things, try to help fix the problem. But do not leave quickly. Like the Christian spouse of an unbelieving person, you might be the very salvation for your church in the area of giving.

10 Write and practice this week's memory verse.

_____

_____

_____

_____

AT THE END OF THE WEEK ANSWER THESE QUESTIONS

What was the most meaningful statement(s) or scripture this week?	Reword the statement or scripture into a prayer of response to God.	What actions do you need to take in response to this week's study?

Always Keep Your Promises

There is a story of a believer named Ananias in the New Testament. He was a member of the first group of Christians that shared everything they had with God for his work. Ananias saw what others were doing and made a commitment. Then things went sideways. Here is how the story goes in.

> The whole congregation of believers was united as one—one heart, one mind! They didn't even claim ownership of their own possessions. No one said, "That's mine; you can't have it." They shared everything. The apostles gave powerful witness to the resurrection of the Master Jesus, and grace was on all of them. And so it turned out that not a person among them was needy. Those who owned fields or houses sold them and brought the price of the sale to the apostles and made an offering of it. The apostles then distributed it according to each person's need.
>
> Joseph, called by the apostles "Barnabas" (which means "Son of Comfort"), a Levite born in Cyprus, sold a field that he owned, brought the money, and made an offering of it to the apostles.
>
> But a man named Ananias—his wife, Sapphira, conniving in this with him—sold a piece of land, secretly kept part of the price for himself, and then brought the rest to the apostles and made an offering of it.
>
> Peter said, "Ananias, how did Satan get you to lie to the Holy Spirit and secretly keep back part of the price of the field? Before you sold it, it was all yours, and after you sold it, the money was yours to do with as you wished. So what got into you to pull a trick like this? You didn't lie to men but to God."
>
> Ananias, when he heard those words, fell down dead. That put the fear of God into everyone who heard of it. The younger men went right to work and wrapped him up, then carried him out and buried him.
>
> Everyone who heard of these things had a healthy respect for God. They knew God was not to be trifled with.
>
> Acts 4:32-5:6, 11 (MSG)

You are part of the church. You chose to follow God. You should be outrageously generous with God. You should tithe. After the tithe, you can decide what to do with the other ninety percent. You should give offerings. You should take care of one another. Hopefully, you will not think of the ninety percent as yours. But whatever you do, you need to keep your word! Too many believers suffer financial and character crises because they withhold their tithe, because they are not generous, and even more because they do not keep their promises. Don't make Ananias' story your story!

TRUTH 13

MEMORY VERSE

Don't collect for yourselves treasures on earth, where moth and rust destroy and where thieves break in and steal. But collect for yourselves treasures in heaven, where neither moth nor rust destroys, and where thieves don't break in and steal. For where your treasure is, there your heart will be also.

Matthew 6:19-21 HCSB

Material Possessions

I Work for Tips

I began working for an hourly wage. Then I worked for a salary. Then I worked for a salary plus bonuses. Then I worked on my own, billing up to $1000 an hour. Now I work for tips.

Well, not really tips, but it is the same thing. I left the corporate world and my consulting business to teach youth about Christ. And, when I started my new journey, my financial world changed. I had to trust God to provide. Like a waiter, I served and trusted that God would provide. That is the deal we made.

The churches I served set a salary for me, but long before I went into full-time ministry, I had seen the disaster of humans and churches. I had seen promises go unfulfilled and disobedience result in unexpected layoffs. I had seen congregations expect ministry folks to live at the poverty level while they lived much better. So I told God, "If we are going to do this, I am not trusting the people to provide. I am trusting you to provide. I work for you, and I trust your promises."

But the perspective that everything I would ever receive came from God challenged me. If everything came from him, if I was relying on him, I better spend it well. And that journey with God has refined me. I have learned the hard way that I don't need everything I think I need. I have become content with less and found joy in not having to manage much. I struggled with self-denial that actually became prideful. I struggled with guilt over spending money on luxuries feeling like I had to explain it to others. I have failed and spent the money God provided on stupid things. But somewhere in all the learning, I found freedom from material stuff. I have learned to enjoy the blessings that come from him. I have learned to live on next to nothing. I have learned to save for a rainy day without feeling bad that others do not.

Perhaps the biggest lesson was that I should have lived this way long before I went into ministry. In all those years of success and growing salary, I should have realized that I was trusting God and that everything was coming from him. I should have known that I was always working for tips. I could have been free from materialism long before I was.

QUICK, SMART START

MATERIALISM

We all tend to trust in wealth and possessions for our security. Even when it has nothing to do with security, we long for more. From the latest iPhone to a new car, we tend to want the next new thing. The desire for material things seems to be rooted deep within us. But, God pushes against this tendency telling us,

> Don't collect for yourselves treasures on earth, where moth and rust destroy and where thieves break in and steal. But collect for yourselves treasures in heaven, where neither moth nor rust destroys, and where thieves don't break in and steal. For where your treasure is, there your heart will be also.
>
> Matthew 6:19-21 HCSB

Materialism is the desire to trust our possessions for security, status, or happiness. Whether or not you have struggled with materialism, there is little doubt that you have experienced it. Advertisers are constantly pitching the next new thing that will improve our life. Celebrities and social media push products that will make us more popular. Have you ever felt like someone was more interested in what you owned or wore than in you? If so, you have encountered materialism. Vocabulary.com provides this description of materialism,

> Materialism describes the belief that buying and having possessions is not just important, but a key to happiness in life, like the people whose materialism has so clouded their minds that they are more interested in your clothes and shoes than in what you are saying.

Collins Dictionary defines materialism as,

> The attitude of someone who attaches a lot of importance to money and wants to possess a lot of material things.

For Christians, materialism is the tendency to consider material possessions and physical comfort more important than spiritual values and contentment.

MATERIAL POSSESSIONS

The flip side of our seemingly endless desires is wondering whether we should have any luxuries. It is natural to become increasingly selfless as you mature in your faith. Do you struggle with owning a great house or car when others are suffering and poor? Have you ever felt guilty about a big purchase? Do you wonder if having luxuries is wrong?

Our ability to have more than we need comes from God (see [Deuteronomy 8:18](#)). God longs for his people to thrive. The Bible is full of truths that teach us how to succeed in life, business, and industry. But God does not just teach us how to live prosperously; sometimes, he causes his people to prosper. Solomon, the third king of Israel, was the wealthiest man of his time because God caused him to prosper.

When Solomon became king, God told him to ask for anything he wanted. Solomon chose wisdom, and God granted his request. The Spirit of God made Solomon the wisest man in history. But, God also gave Solomon riches saying,

> Because your greatest desire is to help your people, and you did not ask for wealth, riches, fame, or even the death of your enemies or a long life, but rather you asked for wisdom and knowledge to properly govern my people—12I will certainly give you the wisdom and knowledge you requested. But I will also give you wealth, riches, and fame such as no other king has had before you or will ever have in the future!
>
> 2 Chronicles 1:11-12

Deuteronomy 8:18

You shall remember the Lord your God, for it is he who gives you power to get wealth

1 Why did God give Solomon riches?

_____

_____

Solomon did not ask anything for himself. He asked for wisdom on how to lead God's people. God rewarded his humility and lack of materialism by giving him great wealth. As Paul was mentoring Timothy to lead a local church, he wrote,

> Teach those who are rich in this world not to be proud and not to trust in their money, which is so unreliable. Their trust should be in God, who richly gives us all we need for our enjoyment. Tell

them to use their money to do good. They should be rich in good works and generous to those in need, always being ready to share with others. By doing this they will be storing up their treasure as a good foundation for the future so that they may experience true life.

1 Timothy 6:17-19

God gives good gifts to his children. He teaches us how to prosper beyond our needs.

Paul warns of the dangers of wealth, but he also recognizes that God,

Richly gives us all we need for our enjoyment.

God often gives us more than we need. He gives to us richly. And, we are allowed to enjoy his blessings. Throughout history, God has made his people wealthy. Again and again, God gives his people more than they need. Having luxuries, wealth, and material possessions is not wrong. James writes,

Whatever is good and perfect is a gift coming down to us from God our Father, who created all the lights in the heavens.

James 1:17

God gives good gifts to his children. He teaches us how to prosper beyond our needs. God promises to bless the work of our hands as we follow his principles and promises. But, he also warns us of the dangers of material wealth.

❷ When do you think having more than we need becomes wrong?

_____

_____

❸ Write and practice this week's memory verse.

_____

_____

_____

CAN MATERIAL POSSESSIONS BE A PROBLEM?

Being prosperous has its challenges. We can quickly shift the focus of our trust and hope from God back to material things. It is a weakness of our old nature of self-reliance. It is easy to forget the source of our blessings. It is easy to become attached to our wealth. And, worst of all, it seems that the more we have, the more we want. Solomon warns us,

> Don't wear yourself out trying to get rich. Be wise enough to know when to quit. In the blink of an eye wealth disappears, for it will sprout wings and fly away like an eagle.
>
> Proverbs 23:4-5

Do you know someone who has to work overtime to support their luxurious lifestyle? Have you heard the tales of older people who wish they had spent more time with their family? Solomon encourages us to stop increasing the need for more money. We so often think, "If I only had a little more..." or "If I only had..." when in reality, we already have enough. It is easy to fall in love with money and possessions, hoping to find a little more peace, a little more rest, or a bit more happiness. Solomon wrote this about our pursuit for more,

> Those who love money will never have enough. How meaningless to think that wealth brings true happiness! The more you have, the more people come to help you spend it. So what good is wealth—except perhaps to watch it slip through your fingers! People who work hard sleep well, whether they eat little or much. But the rich seldom get a good night's sleep.
>
> Ecclesiastes 5:10-12

The truth of the matter is that wealth and prosperity bring more work. The more we have, the more we have to sustain, and the more we seem to worry. I knew a man who took his life because he felt he had "lost everything" during a recession. More disturbing than his suicide was his leaving a million dollars to his spouse. Can you believe it? He was worried about only having a million dollars left!
We struggle with the same loss of perspective regarding material possessions. The more we have, the more we get used to having, and we

reset our worry to a higher level. The older people get, the more they say, "Life was simpler and happier when we had nothing." We know that money does not buy love, happiness, peace, or rest. But, the more we have, the more we tend to forget this truth. There is also a danger that we will begin to measure ourselves by material success instead of spiritual success. Jesus said,

> Beware! Guard against every kind of greed. Life is not measured by how much you own.
> Luke 12:15

Our lives are not measured by what we have. Our lives are measured by who we are and are becoming. As Christians, our character is the ultimate measure of our success. How well are we applying the truths of God to our daily lives? Are we at peace with ourselves and God? Is the Spirit transforming us? Are we better humans? These are the questions that we should be asking when it comes to measuring success. And, none of these virtues can be bought.

Measuring our success by how much we have is the beginning of self-pride and self-reliance. Paul's words to Timothy echo here.

> Teach those who are rich in this world not to be proud and not to trust in their money, which is so unreliable. Their trust should be in God, who richly gives us all we need for our enjoyment.
> 1 Timothy 6:17-19

You can guard against pride by remembering the source of your success. Everything that you own was created by God. Some blessings come unexpectedly, while others result from hard work. But, even the ability and opportunity to work are gifts from God. We prosper because of what God has created.

 Immediately before the Israelites took possession of the land God promised them, he warned his people about the dangers of materialism. Read the passage below and circle the warnings that you find.

> When you have eaten your fill, be sure to praise the Lord your God for the good land he has given you. "But that is the time to be careful! Beware that in your plenty you do not forget the Lord your God and disobey his commands, regulations, and

decrees that I am giving you today. For when you have become full and prosperous and have built fine homes to live in, and when your flocks and herds have become very large and your silver and gold have multiplied along with everything else, be careful! Do not become proud at that time and forget the Lord your God, who rescued you from slavery in the land of Egypt. Do not forget that he led you through the great and terrifying wilderness with its poisonous snakes and scorpions, where it was so hot and dry. He gave you water from the rock! He fed you with manna in the wilderness, a food unknown to your ancestors. He did this to humble you and test you for your own good. He did all this so you would never say to yourself, 'I have achieved this wealth with my own strength and energy.'

Deuteronomy 8:10-17

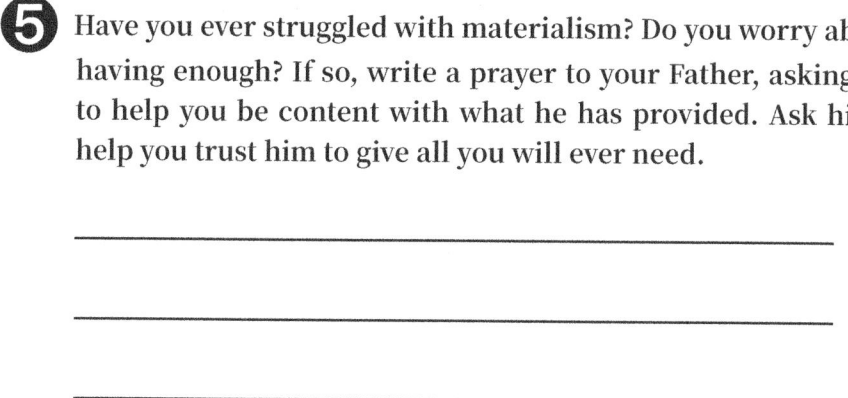

Rejoice in the prosperity that God gives you, but know when enough is enough. Do not let the love of money become your master.

God warned them that having "plenty" could cause them to forget where wealth came from. Plenty could cause them to forget God. Plenty could cause them to feel like they did not need God. Having much could cause self-pride and affect their relationship with God. God never wants his children to say, "I achieved this on my own."

Rejoice in the prosperity that God gives you, but know when enough is enough. Do not let the love of money become your master. Do not let your possessions rule you or steal time from spiritual things.

❺ Have you ever struggled with materialism? Do you worry about having enough? If so, write a prayer to your Father, asking him to help you be content with what he has provided. Ask him to help you trust him to give all you will ever need.

_____

_____

_____

QUICK, SMART START

HOW SHOULD I VIEW MONEY AND POSSESSIONS?

You should view money and possessions as gifts from God to bless you and those around you. No matter how much or how little you have, what you have is a gift from God. Having a good view of material things is being content with what God has provided. Paul told the Philippians that contentment was the secret to his success.

A good view of material things is being content with what God has provided.

> Not that I was ever in need, for I have learned how to be content with whatever I have. I know how to live on almost nothing or with everything. I have learned the secret of living in every situation, whether it is with a full stomach or empty, with plenty or little.
>
> Philippians 4:11-12

Agur writes this wisdom in Proverbs,

> O God, I beg two favors from you; let me have them before I die. First, help me never to tell a lie. Second, give me neither poverty nor riches! Give me just enough to satisfy my needs. For if I grow rich, I may deny you and say, "Who is the Lord?" And if I am too poor, I may steal and thus insult God's holy name.
>
> Proverbs 30:7-9

Now that is wisdom! Agur wanted to honor God. He recognized the danger of forgetting God in wealth or dishonoring God in poverty. His desire was to have what he needed. The tenth commandment reads,

> You must not covet your neighbor's house. You must not covet your neighbor's wife, male or female servant, ox or donkey, or anything else that belongs to your neighbor."
>
> Exodus 20:17

Jealousy over the prosperity of others is dangerous. Have you ever felt that God was cheating you? Have you ever felt like the success of someone else was not fair? Have you ever wished you were them? An Old Testament songwriter penned these words,

So don't be dismayed when the wicked grow rich and their homes become ever more splendid. For when they die, they take nothing with them. Their wealth will not follow them into the grave.

Psalm 49:16-17

The psalm reminds us that material things are only temporary. But more importantly, it reminds us that material wealth will not save anyone. Material wealth is not worth our jealousy. We have eternal life! We have found forgiveness! We are the children of God. Instead of being jealous, we can embrace Paul's encouragement to take it a step further and

Rejoice with those who rejoice

Romans 12:15

Being content with what God has given us allows us to celebrate the prosperity of others (see Psalm 106:5). Cover to cover, the Bible illustrates that a proper view of material possessions begins and ends with contentment.

Psalm 106:5

Let me see the good things you do for your chosen people. Let me be happy along with your happy nation; let me join your own people in praising you.

 Read the verses below and underline the words or phrases about being content with what you have.

Your life should be free from the love of money. Be satisfied with what you have, for He Himself has said, I will never leave you or forsake you.

Hebrews 13:5 HCSB

The Lord is my shepherd; I have all that I need.

Psalm 23:1

If we have food and covering, with these we shall be content.

1 Timothy 6:8 NASB

And this same God who takes care of me will supply all your needs from his glorious riches, which have been given to us in Christ Jesus.

Philippians 4:19

True contentment is a spiritual thing. It begins when we realize that Jesus is our shepherd. Shepherds never leave their flock. They live with their flock. They take care of their flock. If God is for you, rich or poor, how much more could you want? His love, grace, and peace are enough. Spiritual contentment conquers the desire to have more. You do not need more to be happy. You need the peace that surpasses all understanding. You do not need more to have status. You have been accepted by the King of the Universe. You do not need to be jealous. You can celebrate your brother's blessings. At the end of the day, having the basics is enough. The less you have, the simpler your life is. Remember, even in the hard times, your Father loves you and has plenty that he can provide.

7 What material possessions do you need right now to have the basics of food, clothing, and a roof over your head?

_____

_____

Our view of material wealth is that it is a blessing to enjoy and, more importantly, to share with those around us. When Paul warned the rich not to be prideful, he also encouraged them to share the wealth. He echoed Jesus' words about investing in spiritual treasures, writing,

> Tell them to use their money to do good. They should be rich in good works and generous to those in need, always being ready to share with others. By doing this they will be storing up their treasure as a good foundation for the future so that they may experience true life.
>
> 1 Timothy 6:17-19

Keep your life free from the love of money, and be content with what you have, for he has said, "I will never fail you nor forsake you."

8 What material possessions consume more of your time and money that could be freed up to bless God's work and others?

_____

_____

MATERIAL POSSESSIONS

9 Write and practice this week's memory verse.

_____

_____

_____

10 What three steps can you take to protect yourself from materialism?

_____

_____

_____

AT THE END OF THE WEEK ANSWER THESE QUESTIONS

What was the most meaningful statement(s) or scripture this week?	Reword the statement or scripture into a prayer of response to God.	What actions do you need to take in response to this week's study?

TRUTH 14

MEMORY VERSE

And when people escape from the wickedness of the world by knowing our Lord and Savior Jesus Christ and then get tangled up and enslaved by sin again, they are worse off than before.

2 Peter 2:20

Sin

Why O Why Do I Sin?

Do you remember what it was like to sin before you became a follower of Christ? My friend, Nathanael, started following God as a child. I became a follower of Christ in my twenties. He grew up with the rules to do right and avoided most of the awful things I did on my way to Christ. Nathanael was saved from many sins. I was saved out of many sins. Nathanael does not remember what it was like to sin before salvation. I remember him saying, "I think it is easier for you to get the whole sin and grace thing."

The new light was incredible when I became aware of my need and found Christ. Forgiveness was a vivid experience. The new light made my old life disgusting to me. I was distraught when I sinned after salvation. If you became a Christian as an adult, you get Peter's words to the new Christians of his time.

> And when people escape from the wickedness of the world by knowing our Lord and Savior Jesus Christ and then get tangled up and enslaved by sin again, they are worse off than before. It would be better if they had never known the way to righteousness than to know it and then reject the command they were given to live a holy life. They prove the truth of this proverb: "A dog returns to its vomit.
> 2 Peter 2:20-22

I know what that is like. Every time I sin, I am distraught. I never want to go back to doing it my way. I never want to be dirty again. But, stupid me, I still sometimes go back and eat my vomit.

Nathanael may have been missing the stark contrast between the old and new as he grew up, but he gets it now. He grew up. Nathanael started living independently. He began questioning his faith, searching to validate it for his adult self. He made a terrible choice or two. I have watched the Holy Spirit convict Nathanael the same way He convicted me. I have seen his regret, and I hate it for him.

Why is it that we return to the mud puddles in our lives? Why do we do what we know we are going to regret? There is hope. You can know how we sin, why we want to sin, and how you can avoid sin entirely.

QUICK, SMART START

THE ANATOMY OF SIN

Sin is the act of not recognizing and following God's life-saving, life-giving truths. Simply put, followers sin when they do not follow. God is pure and just and sets the standard for holiness. He gives us his Spirit and truths so we can have abundant lives. If we choose God and then do not choose his ways, we deny what we say we believe. That is sin.

One of the most influential books I have read is "The Ten(der) Commandments" by Ron Mehl. The title reveals the big concept of the book. God gave his commandments for our good. He is for us, not against us. He gave his life so that we could thrive in our original design. Jesus told the people,

John 3:17

God sent his Son into the world not to judge the world, but to save the world through him.

> I came that they may have life and have it abundantly. I am the good shepherd. The good shepherd lays down his life for the sheep. He who is a hired hand and not a shepherd, who does not own the sheep, sees the wolf coming and leaves the sheep and flees, and the wolf snatches them and scatters them. He flees because he is a hired hand and cares nothing for the sheep. I lay down my life for the sheep.
>
> John 10:10-13,15 ff ESV

Jesus came to earth to rescue us. He did not come to condemn us (see John 3:17). He came to show us the way back to God. Accepting Christ is a quick, one-time decision that changes our lives forever. We become his children. We are forgiven. Salvation happens in the blink of an eye, but the journey to sin-free living takes longer. Getting our hearts and mind in line with God is a process, and we struggle with sin along the way. It happens. But did you know it always happens in three ways?

There are three ways to sin. You can find them throughout the Old and New Testaments. You can see them in the history of good and bad people. From the beginning of humankind, God has warned us of danger. He has warned us of temptation. He always told his children to "not do" certain things. John put it this way,

> All unrighteousness is sin...
>
> 1 John 5:17 HCSB

The first way to sin is to "do a don't." Anything that does not reflect God's heart and character is the opposite of God. It is a sin. Paul urged new Christians to put away their old lives and embrace their new life (read Romans 6). He urged them to listen to God's Spirit and Word to find abundant life. We get this. The first thing we want to do after salvation is to stop doing the wrong stuff that we were doing. Our first steps in faith are to walk away from the old, but what do we walk towards? God's plan is that we will walk towards the things that are good for us. The same way God has told us not to do certain things, there are other things he has told us to do. And, when we do not follow God in those good things, we also sin. James put it this way,

> Remember, it is sin to know what you ought to do and then not do it.
>
> James 4:17

Salvation happens in the blink of an eye, but the journey to sin-free living takes longer.

The second way to sin is to "not do a do." When we fail to do what we ought to do, we sin by not following God's directions for our good. The third way to sin is a bit more tricky. Paul talked about it with the Romans. His conclusion was,

> If you do anything you believe is not right, you are sinning.
>
> Romans 14:23

Paul was addressing all those things that were not clear. Do we eat meat? Do we go to church on Sunday or another day? What school do we go to? Should we buy a car? Christians have a lot of freedom when it comes to living. You can eat meat. You can be vegan. You can worship on Wednesday. You can worship on Sunday. You are free to have a glass of wine. You are free to abstain. Two Christians can make different choices on these things, and both can follow God. But, Paul concludes that if you are not convinced that something is what God wants you to do, then you are sinning if you do it.

The third way to sin is to "do a doubt." Why? If you doubt whether you are following God, then you are not following God. Even if you guess correctly, you are not following God when you guess. Remember, the simplest definition of sin is not following God. We need to be convinced that what we are doing is what God wants us to do, or our guesses are sins.

There are three ways to sin.

- Do a don't.
- Don't do a do.
- Do a doubt.

But there are also three attitudes that we have when we sin.

- We sin out of ignorance,
- We sin knowing that we are sinning, or
- We sin defiantly.

Have you said to yourself, "Stupid! How did I miss that? How could I not know that was a sin?" You are not alone. Remember, the journey to sin-free living is going to take a lifetime! All along the way, the Holy Spirit will convict you of new "dos" and "don'ts." You will learn new truths from the Bible. We sin out of ignorance when we sin without knowing that our action was a sin. Have hope. God is gracious. He knows what you know and do not know. He is on your side. Sin is sin, but God does not discipline his children for what they do not know. Paul put it this way,

> Yes, people sinned even before the law was given. But it was not counted as sin because there was not yet any law to break.
>
> Romans 5:13

God works with us to get us there. But what about when we sin, knowing we are sinning? When we know better, there is no excuse for our sin. We knew the good God wanted, and we still chose to do it our way. In this case, we are accountable for our actions. God will discipline us if we keep sinning, but his discipline is always loving and always for our long-term good.

 Read the passage from the Bible below and circle the word discipline each time you see it.

And have you forgotten the encouraging words God spoke to you as his children? He said, "My child, don't make light of the Lord's discipline, and don't give up when he corrects you. ⁶For the Lord disciplines those he loves, and he punishes each one he accepts as his child." ⁷As you endure this divine discipline, remember that God is treating you as his own children. Who ever heard of a child who is never disciplined by its father? ⁸If God doesn't discipline you as he does all of his children, it means that you are illegitimate and are not really his children at all. ⁹Since we respected our earthly fathers who disciplined us, shouldn't we submit even more to the discipline of the Father of our spirits, and really live? ¹⁰For our earthly fathers disciplined us for a few years, doing the best they knew how. But God's discipline is always good for us, so that we might share in his holiness. ¹¹No discipline is enjoyable while it is happening—it's painful! But afterward there will be a peaceful harvest of right living for those who are trained in this way.

Hebrews 12:5-11

 Write the truths about God's discipline of his children next to the verse numbers below.

- verse 5 _____

- verse 6 _____

- verse 7 _____

- verse 8 _____

- verse 9 _____

- verse 10 _____

- verse 11 _____

God is gracious. He knows what you know and do not know. He is on your side. Sin is sin, but God does not discipline his children for what they do not know.

You need to take God's discipline seriously. But instead of getting scared, discouraged, or giving up, you need to lean in and learn (verse 5). Discipline is an act of love (verse 6). Discipline and course correction are normal parts of learning (verse 7). If God did not discipline you when you sinned, your relationship with him would not be healthy. He would not be a caring Father (verse 8). The end goal of discipline is not punishment but great living (verse 9). The point is that God's discipline is always for our good. His discipline pushes us to share in his righteousness. He wants us to thrive (verse 10), and there is tremendous spiritual success when we do not give up during discipline (verse 11). God wants us to be safe. He wants us to learn. He wants to protect us. The Holy Spirit will convict us, and God will discipline us until we get it right. And, He does all that for our own good.

The third attitude people have when they sin is an attitude of defiance. There are times when we fall into temptation and do a don't. There are times we wander into selfishness and don't do a do. There are times when impatience causes us to guess and do a doubt. But, defiant sin is different. Defiant sin denies God, opposes his plans, and often works against God's people. The one who sins defiantly knows their action is wrong and could care less. They yell at God, "I do not care!" Their sin is directly against God. God has zero tolerance for defiant sin.

> You shall have one law for him who does anything unintentionally, for him who is native among the sons of Israel and for the alien who sojourns among them. **But the person who does anything defiantly**, whether he is native or an alien, that one is blaspheming the Lord; and that person shall be cut off from among his people. Because he has despised the word of the Lord and has broken His commandment, that person shall be completely cut off; his guilt will be on him.
>
> Number 15:29-31 NASB

So there are three ways we sin, and we always sin with one of three attitudes. Have you ever struggled with the fact that you seem to want to sin?

❸ What are the three ways to sin and the three attitudes of sin?

_____

_____

_____

❹ Write and practice this week's memory verse.

_____

_____

_____

_____

WHY WOULD ANYONE WANT TO SIN AFTER SALVATION?

Do you feel bad when you realize that you have sinned? Do you feel horrible when you fall into temptation? Do you feel conviction and regret after you sin? Great news -- you do not want to sin!

It is easy to explain sinning out of ignorance. The Holy Spirit convicts you, or you learn a new Biblical truth and realize that you sinned. You did not know your action was a sin. You solve it with a quick prayer letting God know you were wrong and asking for His help. You get up, and you move on.

It is more challenging to work through sins that we do intentionally. How can we say that we do not want to sin when we do something that we know was a sin? It gets even more troubling when you repeat the same sin again and again. You feel like an addict. You feel like a hypocrite. Habitual sin can destroy your spiritual self-confidence. You might even wonder if you are saved. Paul shared his struggle with these feelings.

> I do not understand the things I do. I do not do what I want to do, and I do the things I hate. And if I do not want to do the hated things I do, that means I agree that the law is good... I want to do the things that are good, but I do not do them. I do not do the good things I want to do, but I do the bad things I do not want to do... In my mind, I am happy with God's law. But I see another law working in my body, which makes war against the law that my mind accepts. That other law working in my body is the law of sin, and it makes me its prisoner. What a miserable man I am! Who will save me from this body that brings me death?
>
> Romans 7:15-16,18b-19,22b-24 NCV

Have you ever felt that way? You really want to follow God. You agree that His ways are best. You really want to do what God wants you to do. But you do don'ts and don't do do's! It is a horrible feeling.

Paul explained why we struggle with sinning even though we do not want to sin. He realized that he was in a battle between his new life and his old ways, old thoughts, and old temptations. Here is his explanation,

> But I am not really the one who is doing these hated things; it is sin living in me that does them. Yes, I know that nothing good lives in me—I mean nothing good lives in the part of me that is earthly and sinful. I want to do the things that are good, but I do not do them...So if I do things I do not want to do, then I am not the one doing them. It is sin living in me that does those things.
>
> So I have learned this rule: When I want to do good, evil is there with me. In my mind, I am happy with God's law. But I see another law working in my body, which makes war against the law that my mind accepts.
>
> Romans 7:17-18,21-23 NCV

Paul realized that he was living in a body corrupted by sin. He realized that as long as he was on earth, he would struggle against the sin in his flesh. He even recognized that sin had a way of tricking him into wanting to sin. Have you suddenly wanted to do something after someone told you it was wrong? Paul did.

> I would never have known what it means to want to take something belonging to someone else if the law had not said, "You must not want to take your neighbor's things." And sin found a way to use that command and cause me to want all kinds of things I should not want. But without the law, sin has no power. I was alive before I knew the law. But when the law's command came to me, then sin began to live, and I died. The command was meant to bring life, but for me it brought death. Sin found a way to fool me by using the command to make me die.
>
> Romans 7:7-11 NCV

God's commands lead us into great living, but somehow sin twists the awareness of sin to get us to want to sin. When someone tells us not to do something, temptation can rise up in us. It is like we are hardwired to rebel against authority and instruction. We struggle with someone telling us what to do. We struggle with control issues. Paul wrote, "Once someone told me it was wrong, all the sudden, I wanted to do it." James explains another reason we sin when we really do not want to sin.

> No one undergoing a trial should say, "I am being tempted by God." For God is not tempted by evil, and He Himself doesn't tempt anyone. But each person is tempted when he is drawn away and enticed by his own evil desires. Then after desire has conceived, it gives birth to sin, and when sin is fully grown, it gives birth to death.
>
> James 1:13-15 HCSB

Our old desires can entice us and trick us. Our minds remember having fun when we did something that we now know is sin. The problem is that sin is not fun anymore. The act might be fun, but the conviction afterward is not. We can also face direct temptations when we dwell on things that are not good for us.

Mike, the first minister who reached me, used to tell the guys, "The first look at a sexy girl is not sinning. It's not even the second or third look that's sin. You are supposed to be attracted to her. It is natural. You are headed towards sin when desire rises in you, but you still have not sinned. You get closer to sinning the more you dwell on the lust. The further you go in your mind, the closer you are to acting out a sin. If the desire can draw you away from listening to God, sin is right around the corner.

Mike encouraged us to pray our brains out and think ahead to the inevitable regret we would feel. He encouraged us to replace desire with thoughts of respect, looking at the girl as our sister in Christ. Mike was trying to get us to derail the train of uncontrolled, improper desire.

James and Mike agree. Whether the object of our desire is self-respect, power, sex, or even cheesecake, we are tempted to sin when our desire draws us away from God's character, truths, and ways. If we dwell on those desires long enough, we often act on them. We sin. We follow our desire instead of God's. And, just like in the garden, just like Paul experienced, sin "kills" us (see Romans 8:7-8). Sin disconnects us from God's Spirit (see 1 Thessalonians 5:19). Sin simply gets in God's way.

> *No follower of Christ wants to sin. We sin in the moment because we fall into the same traps as all the children of God before us.*

❺ Do you have any lingering sin that you keep wrestling with? If you do, take a minute and ask God for help. Ask him to have his Spirit begin to work deep inside you to erase the old desire and replace it with a new desire. Ask God, "What is the opposite of my sin that will bring joy instead of regret?"

_____

No follower of Christ wants to sin. We sin in the moment because we fall into the same traps as all the children of God before us. We dwell on desires from the old life. We get tricked by the enemy and our past. We sin because our old self does not want to be told, "No." Are you wondering if there is any hope? Is there a way to stop the madness? There is. It is actually possible to not sin.

QUICK, SMART START

DO WE HAVE TO SIN?

No one has to sin. We all have the freedom to choose right and wrong. Even unbelieving people can choose. Paul wrote this about unbelieving people.

> Even Gentiles, who do not have God's written law, show that they know his law when they instinctively obey it, even without having heard it. They demonstrate that God's law is written in their hearts, for their own conscience and thoughts either accuse them or tell them they are doing right.
>
> Romans 2:14-15

When God established the nation of Israel (in the Old Testament), he gave the Israelites specific instructions on how to live. These truths, these commands, became known as the Law. The Ten Commandments, like do not murder and do not commit adultery, were part of the law. But the law addressed everything. It even included a complete legal system for handling disputes. If you knew the law, you knew God's desire for humankind. You knew exactly what to do and what not to do. Even if you did not want to follow God's law, you were held accountable because you had no excuse. You knew what to do. The people who were not Israelites were called Gentiles. The Israelites had the law, but the Gentiles did not have the law.

So what was Paul teaching? Paul said that even those who did not grow up knowing the law still knew the difference between right and wrong. They may not have read the specific instructions, but intuitively, they knew right from wrong. Paul explains that this knowledge of right and wrong was written on their hearts.

> "This is the new covenant I will make with my people on that day, says the Lord: I will put my laws in their hearts, and I will write them on their minds."
>
> Hebrews 10:16-17

John Piper, in his article "How is the Law Written on Every Heart", explains this passage, writing,

> Now, the point here is that Christ has purchased the new covenant promise, and it includes the forgiveness of our sins and the replacement of an old, unbelieving, rebellious heart with a new heart of faith and obedience.

So the Israelites had the law, and the Gentiles intuitively knew what was right from wrong. But Piper notes that followers of Christ have something more. Christians not only have access to God's truths and the intuitive knowledge of right and wrong; Christians have new life. When you believed in God, he made you a new creature. He restored your heart and spirit by putting his Spirit inside you. The essence of who you are has been changed. You are not just an Israelite following the law out of fear without a choice. You are not just a Gentile with a sense of what is right. You chose to follow God, and that choice plus God's Spirit in you results in a desire to follow his ways.

Christians desire to follow God and are empowered to do just that. The Spirit of God warns us when something wrong is going on. He shows us our errors when we are ignorant. He reminds us that something is not right before we sin.

 Read Jesus' words below and circle the two things the Spirit does for those who follow Christ.

> But when the Father sends the Advocate as my representative—that is, the Holy Spirit—he will teach you everything and will remind you of everything I have told you.
>
> John 14:26

The Spirit encourages us to do what is right. The Spirit turns our doubts into a surefire direction.

The Spirit reminds us of everything that God has taught us. He reminds us of God's commands and desires for good living that we have read in the Bible. He reminds us of what God has told us to do and not to do. But the Spirit also continues to teach us. God's Spirit helps us know what to do even when there is no direct instruction in the Bible.

The Spirit encourages us to do what is right. The Spirit turns our doubts into a surefire direction. The Spirit reveals temptations that are gaining ground in our lives. The Spirit is our early warning system when it comes to following God. The book of Hebrews reminds us that God understands what we face as desires rise and when Satan deceives.

> For we do not have a high priest who is unable to sympathize with our weaknesses, but One who has been tested in every way as we are, yet without sin. Therefore let us approach the throne of grace with boldness, so that we may receive mercy and find grace to help us at the proper time.
>
> Hebrews 4:15 HCSB

Jesus was tested in real life, and he did not sin. He can sympathize with our challenges. His experience provides hope that there is a way out and a way not to sin. His Spirit is there with mercy and strength to help us. We only need to ask. Do you see it?

- You desire to follow God because you have a new heart.
- You know God's instructions for successful living because you have the Bible.
- You have the intuition to know right from wrong because God has given everyone that ability by his design.
- You can know what to do when there is no direct Biblical answer because you have the Spirit of God to guide you.

But you also have the power, mercy, and grace to help you follow. God gives you supernatural strength if you only ask him for help. Paul's words encourage us to remember God is on our side and there to help.

The simplest definition of sin is not follow God. The simplest way out of sin is to follow Him.

> The only temptation that has come to you is that which everyone has. But you can trust God, who will not permit you to be tempted more than you can stand. But when you are tempted, he will also give you a way to escape so that you will be able to stand it.
>
> 1 Corinthians 10:13 NCV

The incredible truth is that you do not have to sin. It may seem too simple, but choosing God is good, and choosing Him results in you not sinning. He will never allow you to be trapped. He is God. He is powerful.

The simplest definition of sin is not follow God. The simplest way out of sin is to follow Him. We can execute an immediate course correction when the Holy Spirit says, "Do this," or "Don't do that." And, we can ask for the strength that we do not feel we have.

❼ Write and practice this week's memory verse.

_____

_____

_____

SIN

HOW CAN I AVOID SINNING?

You do not have to sin! There is always a way out of sinning. And the most effective solution comes long before the challenge.

Brushing, flossing, and dentist visits are the best ways to prevent cavities and gum disease. Flossing removes plaque that leads to bad breath and decay. Avoiding the temptation to chew ice prevents the most common reason teeth chip and crack. Preventative dentistry is the best way to keep a healthy smile. And preventative living is the best way to have a healthy Christian journey.

The best strategy to avoid sin is to pursue good. Think about it. If you spend all day doing what is good in God's eyes, there is little time left for sin. The more time you spend doing what is right and good, the less exposure you have to temptation. But there are some practical steps that you can take to protect yourself.

Right Place, Right Time

My dad always warned me not to be in the wrong place at the wrong time. I remember calling him from the hospital after I got beat up at a rodeo. He listened to my story and said, "Doug. You have to stop being at the wrong place at the wrong time. What were you thinking about hanging out with a bunch of drunk cowboys?" His tough lesson still rings clear in my mind. I have so often been in the wrong place at the wrong time. I have hung out with gossips. I have jumped into conversations I should not have. And, I have put myself in stupid situations that I knew would tempt me. It is only logical to stay away from places, people, and things that could tempt you to walk toward the flesh and away from God (see Ephesians 5:6-17). We should not love the world (see James 4:4), and we should not join ourselves with those who are not his.

> You are not the same as those who do not believe. So do not join yourselves to them. Good and bad do not belong together. Light and darkness cannot share together.
> 2 Corinthians 6:14 NCV

One of the simplest things you can do is be honest about your past sins and make a course correction towards being at the right place at the

James 4:4

Don't you realize that friendship with the world makes you an enemy of God? I say it again: If you want to be a friend of the world, you make yourself an enemy of God.

right time. Solomon had it right when he warned us to be honest about our weaknesses and reject our old ways.

> You will never correct anything until you accept responsibility for your sin. If you hide your sins, you will not succeed. If you confess and reject them, you will receive mercy.
>
> Proverbs 28:13 NCV

Take Control of Your Mind

Temptation happens in two ways: it comes from the outside, or it comes from the inside. In every case, we have to think about whatever is tempting us. We have to give the thought space in our minds. Do you remember what James revealed about how sin happens? Sin always follows temptation, and temptation always follows us dwelling on a desire.

Think about the last time you were tempted to eat cheesecake, have sex, or whatever is a sin to you. It is always about what we see, hear, or remember. Something has to trigger a desire that we can dwell on. The information has to get into our brains for the first time, or it has to be recalled. We cannot dwell on what we do not think about. Step one is being in the right place at the right time, but we cannot always control where we are.

If cheesecake is your sin, you can avoid New York delis and the Cheesecake Factory. But what do you do when you go to a small group, and your host has a delicious cheesecake with fresh strawberry compote? You could leave. You could throw the cake out the window. You could also control your mind. You can remember how you feel after you eat cheesecake. You could remember why cheesecake is a sin for you. You could make the desire submit to reason. I can hear you quietly saying, "Cheesecake does not control me. God in me is bigger than cheesecake." Taking control of your mind is the second line of defense in defeating sin in your life. Paul taught this second strategy to the Christians in Corinth, saying,

> We capture every thought and make it give up and obey Christ.
>
> 2 Corinthians 10:5 NCV

Have you ever cried, "Uncle," when your big brother had you pinned down with spit dangling over your face? We need to pin sin down and make it cry, "Uncle." We need to realize that with God's Spirit, we are no longer slaves to sin. We are more powerful. We do not have to sin. When quitting a particularly controlling habit, I turned to kneeling and praying

---

Ephesians 5:6-8

Don't be fooled by those who try to excuse these sins, for the anger of God will fall on all who disobey him. Don't participate in the things these people do. For once you were full of darkness, but now you have light from the Lord. So live as people of light!

each time I was tempted. I could not seem to avoid the desire, but I could definitely pray. You should have seen me kneeling outside my car, praying for strength. It worked. Each time I paused to pray, I would remember who I wanted to be, and God's Spirit would make me stronger.

When you cannot avoid temptation, control your thoughts. As you control your thoughts, remember where you came from and focus on the future.

Focus on the Future

Jewish people grew up hearing about God. It was part of their history. Even if they did not choose to follow God, they knew about God. They listened to the stories of how God provided for their ancestors. They knew the promises of God. They had a past with God. If they strayed, they had a target of the "good old days" they could return to.

Paul's ministry was focused on the Gentiles, the people who were not Jewish. The Gentiles knew very little about God. Knowing God and worshipping God was not part of their history. There was no "good past" to which to return. So, Paul urged them to point themselves toward the future. He urged them to remember the emptiness of their past and move forward with their new life. He taught them to focus their thoughts on the future.

> Since you were raised from the dead with Christ, aim at what is in heaven, where Christ is sitting at the right hand of God. Think only about the things in heaven, not the things on earth. Your old sinful self has died, and your new life is kept with Christ in God. Christ is your life, and when he comes again, you will share in his glory.
>
> Colossians 3:1-4 NCV

The first strategy to defeat sin is to be in the right place at the right time. The second is to control your thoughts with the help of the Spirit of God. The third strategy is keeping your eye on where you want to be in a week, a month, in five years, or for eternity. Paul taught the Romans,

> But clothe yourselves with the Lord Jesus Christ and forget about satisfying your sinful self.
>
> Romans 13:14 NCV

We can defeat sin by focusing on God rather than the here and now. We can think spiritually. We can point our minds towards the future that God has given us. We can live for that future inheritance. Peter cheered on the new believers writing,

> All praise to God, the Father of our Lord Jesus Christ. It is by his great mercy that we have been born again, because God raised Jesus Christ from the dead. Now we live with great expectation, and we have a priceless inheritance—an inheritance that is kept in heaven for you, pure and undefiled, beyond the reach of change and decay. And through your faith, God is protecting you by his power until you receive this salvation, which is ready to be revealed on the last day for all to see. So be truly glad. There is wonderful joy ahead, even though you must endure many trials for a little while. These trials will show that your faith is genuine.
>
> 1 Peter 1:2-6

Saving money without a goal is difficult. But saving to get that new phone, that new car, or for your future retirement is easier. The value of a better future can prevent us from wasting our money on things that will end up in a garage sale in a year or two. Our faith will be tried. Temptations will come. We will struggle to get our flesh to follow our hearts. But, living with great expectations of what is to come and investing in our spiritual future provides fuel to defeat sin.

Consume Truth

The fourth strategy to defeat sin is consuming God's truths. It empowers the first three strategies. God's truths teach us what sin is; thus, we know what to avoid. God's words teach us what is good. With truth, we can be in the right place at the right time. God's words help us control our thoughts. They provide hope, direction, and promises to dwell on. And God's words describe our incredible future and the great life we can live right now. We find encouragement in the successes of those who followed God and overcame sin. A warning can be found in the failures of humankind. Even more, you can know what is good by getting to know God's character. A songwriter in the Old Testament wrote,

> How can a young person live a pure life? By obeying your word. With all my heart I try to obey you. Don't let me break your commands. I have taken your words to heart so I would not sin against you.
>
> Psalm 119:9-11 NCV

Storing God's truths in your heart and mind should be your first goal if you are new to following God. They are the fuel the Holy Spirit will use to guide you toward all things that are good and right.

When Jesus faced temptation, he quoted the Bible in defense (see Matthew 4:3-11). You can do nothing better than become informed of God's character, directions, and promises by consuming the Bible cover-to-cover.

8 What are the three ways to sin?

_____

_____

_____

9 What are the three attitudes of sinning?

_____

_____

_____

10 Write and practice this week's memory verse?

_____

_____

_____

_____

AT THE END OF THE WEEK ANSWER THESE QUESTIONS

What was the most meaningful statement(s) or scripture this week?	Reword the statement or scripture into a prayer of response to God.	What actions do you need to take in response to this week's study?

TRUTH 15

MEMORY VERSE

Yet we know that a person is made right with God not by following the law, but by trusting in Jesus Christ.

Galatians 2:16 NCV

Free from Judgement

Free to Follow

A disciple once told me, "I stopped smoking pot because I have to take regular drug tests. If I did not have to take the test, I would still be smoking pot!" I pushed back and asked, "But what about the Biblical truth that we should obey the laws of the land? Marijuana is illegal."

"Well, if it became legal. I would probably smoke it," he replied.
"So, why does your job not want you to smoke pot?" I asked.
"Uh…"
"Do you think that they are worried about the impact on quality or your safety?"
"Well, I would not go to work high," he said.
"Okay. So if it would impair your work, wouldn't it also impair your parenting?"
"Uh…"
"Let me tell you why I won't smoke pot again. I love hearing from God, and pot would interrupt that process. I would miss the Holy Spirit and, without a doubt, miss out on an opportunity."

I am no super spiritual guy. In fact, I am just the opposite. I tried living on my own. I failed. Then I found God. I found that God's truths help me succeed at living. I know that I will go to heaven no matter what I do, but that doesn't mean I will live heaven on earth if I ignore God commands. I have found that every decision counts. Every decision reveals whether I have faith in Jesus or not.

Believing in Jesus is like believing that a chair will hold you up. You don't really believe until you sit in the chair. Maybe that is why Jesus said those that love him would follow His commands. It is not that you have to follow to be saved. Instead, if you really believe you will follow. Why wouldn't you?

QUICK, SMART START

JUDGED BY FAITH, NOT WORKS

Salvation is a matter of belief, a matter of faith. Jesus forgave all our past, present, and future sins when he offered his life on the cross.

Since the beginning of time, people have become followers of God in the same way — by believing in him. Faith is the only thing required to become one of God's children. Before Jesus came to earth, people exhibited their faith by hoping for a future savior and following God's ways. In essence, they were looking towards the cross. They were waiting for the Messiah, Jesus, who would sacrifice himself to pay the penalty for all sin. After Jesus, we look back at that same cross of forgiveness. We exhibit our faith by believing in that cross, that Savior, and following God's ways. Their faith in waiting on the Savior is the same as our faith in looking back to a Savior.

Before Jesus' sacrifice on the cross, humans were judged by their actions. Humans were judged by what they did because what they did exposed who they believed in. When people followed God's ways, it demonstrated that they believed in God. Their belief made them righteous. Today, we are judged the same way. We are judged by who we believe in. Confessing Jesus Christ as our savior demonstrates who we believe in.

Jesus brought complete forgiveness to the world. To the ones who believed before he came and those who believed after he came. Anyone who believed or believes is deemed righteous regardless of their actions. Salvation is a matter of belief, a matter of faith. Jesus forgave all our past, present, and future sins when he offered his life on the cross.

> But our High Priest offered himself to God as a single sacrifice for sins, good for all time. For by that one offering he forever made perfect those who are being made holy.
>
> Hebrews 10:12,14

1 How many offerings are required for people to be made holy?

_____

_____

FREE FROM JUDGEMENT

Only one offering needs to be made, and it was made by Jesus. Our behavior no longer determines our destination. We are free from judgment because Jesus judged us as righteous the moment we believed. Paul explains,

> Yet we know that a person is made right with God not by following the law, but by trusting in Jesus Christ. So we, too, have put our faith in Christ Jesus, that we might be made right with God because we trusted in Christ. It is not because we followed the law, because no one can be made right with God by following the law.
>
> Galatians 2:16 NCV

You are no longer judged by the law, but God's truths still apply. You are free, but you are not free to do whatever you want.

Jesus' sacrifice has set us free from being judged by our actions. But many people try to twist that freedom. They think they can do whatever they want and be okay with God. Paul pushed back on this idea, writing,

> For you have been called to live in freedom, my brothers and sisters. But don't use your freedom to satisfy your sinful nature. Instead, use your freedom to serve one another in love.
>
> Galatians 5:13

> You say, "I am allowed to do anything"—but not everything is good for you... But you can't say that our bodies were made for sexual immorality.
>
> 1 Corinthians 6:12,13

You are no longer judged by the law, but God's truths still apply. You are free, but you are not free to do whatever you want. How much of the law should you follow? What does it mean to be free from judgment? Can you do anything and get to heaven? Are there consequences for your behavior? Let's look at what the Bible says about the balance between freedom from the Law and being a responsibly acting child of God.

❷ Write and memorize this week's memory verse.

_____

_____

_____

QUICK, SMART START

AM I FREE TO DO WHATEVER I WANT?

Clearly, you are free to make your own choices, even wrong ones. God created humans with the unique ability to choose. And you chose God. You became a believer. You were saved by faith. You are righteous because Jesus has made you righteous. You are no longer judged by your actions. Even if your actions stink, you will end up in heaven because you chose to believe in God.

But when Jesus set you free from the law, he did not set you free to do whatever you want. He set you free so that you could follow, thrive, and live an abundant life. God never intended for you to ignore the laws and commands in the Old Testament. God never intended for you to do whatever you wanted to do. Some Christians say, "Jesus fulfilled the law. So it doesn't apply to me. I do not have to keep it." Jesus never said that. In fact, Jesus said the exact opposite.

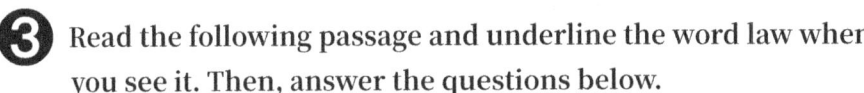 Read the following passage and underline the word law when you see it. Then, answer the questions below.

"Don't misunderstand why I have come. I did not come to abolish the law of Moses or the writings of the prophets. No, I came to accomplish their purpose. ¹⁸I tell you the truth, until heaven and earth disappear, not even the smallest detail of God's law will disappear until its purpose is achieved. ¹⁹So if you ignore the least commandment and teach others to do the same, you will be called the least in the Kingdom of Heaven. But anyone who obeys God's laws and teaches them will be called great in the Kingdom of Heaven. ²⁰ "But I warn you—unless your righteousness is better than the righteousness of the teachers of religious law and the Pharisees, you will never enter the Kingdom of Heaven!

Matthew 5:17-20

Did Jesus abolish the law (verse 17)?

_____

FREE FROM JUDGEMENT

When will the law become invalid (verse 18)?

_____

Are God's commands still good for us today (verse 18)?

_____

What will God call those that ignore his commands in the Old Testament (verse 19)?

_____

How righteous do you have to be to get into heaven (verse 20)?

_____

Jesus did not abolish the law. He kept it (or fulfilled it). He achieved the purpose of the law - complete righteousness. Jesus taught that God's commands are still relevant and useful in our lives. God's commands have a purpose to guide us into righteous living. Everyone who believes gets into heaven. But the one who ignores his commands will be the least in the Kingdom. While Jesus affirms salvation by faith, he elevates the importance of following and keeping God's commands.

Before we knew God, we were slaves to our own ways. Paul tells us that we were slaves to sin. It is like we were owned by our own thoughts and desires. We were the king of our own castle, for good or bad. But when we became Christians, we asked God to become the king of our lives. We may be free to do whatever we want and still get to heaven, but that argument does not make sense. Paul says it this way,

> So, do not let sin control your life here on earth so that you do what your sinful self wants to do. Do not offer the parts of your body to serve sin, as things to be used in doing evil. Instead, offer yourselves to God as people who have died and now live. Offer the parts of your body to God to be used in doing good. Sin will not be your master, because you are not under law but under God's grace. So what should we do? Should we sin because we are under grace and not under law? No! Surely you know that when you give yourselves like slaves to obey someone, then you are really slaves of that person. The person you obey is your master. You can follow sin, which brings spiritual death, or you can obey God, which makes you right with him. In the past you were slaves to sin—sin controlled you. But thank God, you fully obeyed the things that you were taught. You were made free from sin, and now you are slaves to goodness.
>
> Romans 6:12-18 NCV

The greatness of freedom in Christ is not found in the ability to do whatever you want. The distinction of freedom in Christ is that you are free to never sin again. You are free from being controlled by the world and the flesh. You are free from judgment and free to start following God's ways of incredible living. Jesus was teaching a group of Jewish people about freedom when he said,

> You are truly my disciples if you remain faithful to my teachings. And you will know the truth, and the truth will set you free.
> John 8:31-32

You are free from being controlled by the world and the flesh. You are free from judgment and free to start following God's ways of incredible living.

They questioned him, saying,

> We are Abraham's children, and we have never been anyone's slaves. So why do you say we will be free?"

Here is Jesus' answer.

> I tell you the truth, everyone who lives in sin is a slave to sin. A slave does not stay with a family forever, but a son belongs to the family forever. So if the Son makes you free, you will be truly free.
> John 8:33-36 NCV

Many people miss the beauty of the freedom God gives. We could not follow Christ before we were saved. But now, because we are believers -- filled with the Spirit, forgiven, reborn, and with a new nature -- we can follow Christ. Peter said it excellently,

> Live as free people, but do not use your freedom as an excuse to do evil. Live as servants of God. Show respect for all people: Love the brothers and sisters of God's family, respect God, honor the king.
> 1 Peter 2:16 NCV

You are free to do whatever you choose. Use your freedom to serve your Living God!

4 How faithful are you to God's teachings? Are you a disciple?

_____

_____

5 Are there any areas where your freedom is an excuse to do something that is not part of God's smart plan for living?

_____

_____

HOW DO MY FREE CHOICES AFFECT MY LIFE?

Day 3

Every decision we make counts. Every decision moves us forward or back in our journey of faith. Every choice has consequences. Poor choices slow our spiritual growth, disconnect us from God, and create drama in our world. Good decisions bring peace, mercy, strength, and a great relationship with your Father. But perhaps the best consequence of following God is the ability to be used for special purposes.

> "...The Lord knows those who belong to him," and "Everyone who wants to belong to the Lord must stop doing wrong." In a large house there are not only things made of gold and silver, but also things made of wood and clay. Some things are used for special purposes, and others are made for ordinary jobs. **All who make themselves clean from evil will be used for special purposes**. They will be made holy, useful to the Master, ready to do any good work.
>
> 2 Timothy 2:19-21 NCV

So many of my peers have already settled into deck chairs by the pool of life. They are enjoying grandkids and going on cruises. Other friends are working hard to make a future doing what they are expected to do. They are all living normal lives, and that is okay. Normal is not bad; normal is just the killer of special. How great would it be to be used by God to do

QUICK, SMART START

something special? One of my personal goals is to stay super healthy as I grow older. I want to be able to go and help people around the world. I want to be able to pick up lumber. I want to be able to dig holes. I want to be able to hike long distances. If I am healthy, I can still sit by the pool, but I will also be ready and able to leap tall buildings and lift cars. Being super healthy spiritually is also one of my goals. I want to be able to provide wisdom, comfort, and teaching. I want to be ready for God's special forces assignments.

5 On a scale of 1 to 10, 10 being the most prepared, how prepared are you for a special God assignment?

_____

_____

6 Do you want to do something God special? Why or why not?

_____

_____

_____

Every decision we make counts. Every decision moves us forward or back in our journey of faith. Every choice has consequences.

You are free to make your own choices. You can choose to rid yourself of evil and fill yourself with God's truths and Spirit. You can choose to be ready to live an awe-inspiring life. Or, you can choose to sin and do your own thing. Either way, be aware of the consequences. A vinedresser keeps his vineyard healthy by pruning the grapevines. He prunes back healthy growth so the vine will be thick. He cuts off dead branches because, well, they are dead. Jesus used the illustration of him being the vine and us being the branches. God was the vinedresser.

7 In Jesus' illustration below, underline the word "branch" or "branches." Circle every word that represents Jesus.

"I am the true vine, and my Father is the vinedresser. Every branch in me that does not bear fruit he takes away, and every branch that does bear fruit he prunes, that it may bear more fruit. Already you are clean because of the word that I have spoken to you. Abide in me, and I in you. As the branch cannot bear fruit by itself, unless it abides in the vine, neither can you, unless you abide in me. I am the vine; you are the branches.

> Whoever abides in me and I in him, he it is that bears much fruit, for apart from me you can do nothing. If anyone does not abide in me he is thrown away like a branch and withers; and the branches are gathered, thrown into the fire, and burned.
>
> John 15:1-6 ESV

Jesus is the vine. You are the branch. You will never be a burned branch because you are a believer. God has set you free from judgment. You will never be thrown away. If you abide in him, you will bear fruit. You will grow spiritually, share with others, love, and be full of the fruit of the Spirit (see Galatians 5:22-23). Did you notice that God prunes the branches that bear fruit? Even if you are producing tons of fruit, God will prune you so that you can bear more fruit. Vinedressers do this all the time. Three clumps of grapes are often pruned to one or two clusters so the remaining clusters will be richer and more robust. In the same way, God will test you, push you, and allow trials to take you deeper and further in your spiritual walk. Pruning like this is not discipline; it is refinement.

There is, however, a pruning that is discipline. God is committed to you bearing fruit and will prune out things that should not be a part of your life and character. He will discipline you so that you can course correct and bear more fruit. The writer of Hebrews encourages us to take this type of God's pruning seriously. He encourages us to embrace it and grow.

> And have you forgotten the encouraging words God spoke to you as his children? He said, "My child, don't make light of the Lord's discipline, and don't give up when he corrects you. For the Lord disciplines those he loves, and he punishes each one he accepts as his child." As you endure this divine discipline, remember that God is treating you as his own children. Who ever heard of a child who is never disciplined by its father? If God doesn't discipline you as he does all of his children, it means that you are illegitimate and are not really his children at all. Since we respected our earthly fathers who disciplined us, shouldn't we submit even more to the discipline of the Father of our spirits, and live forever?
>
> Hebrews 12:5-11

The effects of good and bad choices are like farming. Farmers who plant weeds get weeds. Farmers who plant wheat get wheat. It is the same in the spiritual fields of our souls. If we choose good, good will multiply in

Galatians 5:22-23

But the Holy Spirit produces this kind of fruit in our lives: love, joy, peace, patience, kindness, goodness, faithfulness, gentleness, and self-control.

QUICK, SMART START

our lives. If we choose wrong, trouble will ruin us. God allows us to reap what we sow. Paul taught it this way,

> Do not be fooled: You cannot cheat God. People harvest only what they plant. If they plant to satisfy their sinful selves, their sinful selves will bring them ruin. But if they plant to please the Spirit, they will receive eternal life from the Spirit.
>
> Galatians 6:7-8 NCV

Romans 8:28

And we know that God causes everything to work together for the good of those who love God and are called according to his purpose for them.

Every decision we make counts. Every decision has consequences. So make decisions that produce the life that God intended for you to have. Make decisions today that help you thrive tomorrow. Make decisions that get you ready to go on a special assignment with God.

❽ Are you suffering any negative consequences from poor choices? Read **Romans 8:28** and write a prayer asking God to use your circumstance for good.

_____

_____

_____

FREEDOM IN THE GRAY AREAS OF LIFE

Some decisions are simple because the Bible gives clear direction. For example, the Bible says, "don't murder" (see Exodus 20:13). Even though God can forgive you for murder, you should not murder. The Bible says, "read the Bible"; it is good for you (see 2 Timothy 3:16). So you should read it even though you will not die if you do not read it. But what about the "gray areas" not discussed in the Bible? How do you choose a job? Many Bible characters chose their careers, but sometimes God had a preference. Sometimes he called people to be kings or carpenters. Can you drink wine? Jesus made wine, but the Bible instructs believers to not get drunk. How do you balance your freedom with God's truths and the needs of others? Here are some quick Biblical tips and ideas to help you in these cases:

Avoid things that trip others up.

> For that reason we should stop judging each other. We must make up our minds not to do anything that will make another Christian sin. I am in the Lord Jesus, and I know that there is no food that is wrong to eat. But if a person believes something is wrong, that thing is wrong for him. If you hurt your brother's or sister's faith because of something you eat, you are not really following the way of love. Do not destroy someone's faith by eating food he thinks is wrong, because Christ died for him.
> Romans 14:13-15 NCV

> Never do anything that might hurt others—Jews, Greeks, or God's church— just as I, also, try to please everybody in every way. I am not trying to do what is good for me but what is good for most people so they can be saved.
> 1 Corinthians 10:32-33 NCV

Make choices that make those around you better.

> "We are allowed to do all things," but not all things are good for us to do. "We are allowed to do all things," but not all things help others grow stronger.
> 1 Corinthians 10:23 NCV

Avoid things that appear wrong even though they may not be wrong.

> Do not allow what you think is good to become what others say is evil.
> Romans 14:16 NCV

> Keep what is good, and stay away from everything that is evil.
> 1 Thessalonians 5:21-22 NCV

Make choices that God will bless.

> Everything you do or say should be done to obey Jesus your Lord. And in all you do, give thanks to God the Father through Jesus.
>
> Colossians 3:17 NCV

Don't let anything control you.

> Keep a clear conscience so that those who speak evil of your good life in Christ will be made ashamed.
>
> 1 Peter 3:16 NCV

> "I am allowed to do all things," but not all things are good for me to do. "I am allowed to do all things," but I will not let anything make me its slave.
>
> 1 Corinthians 6:12 NCV

Even if it is not wrong, like cheesecake, smoking, or working out, do not let anything become your master. Embrace balance in your choices. Do not make others stumble. Do not try to impress or win people over with your choices. Your goal in your freedom is to please God, not man. Paul explained this concept to the Galatian believers, writing,

> Do you think I am trying to make people accept me? No, God is the One I am trying to please. Am I trying to please people? If I still wanted to please people, I would not be a servant of Christ.
>
> Galatians 1:10 NCV

Use your freedom for good. Use your freedom to follow God. Use your freedom to become more like Christ. Desire the right thing, the best thing. The writer of Hebrews requests the prayers of his readers, saying,

> Pray for us. We are sure that we have a clear conscience, because we always want to do the right thing.
>
> Hebrews 13:18 NCV

Your freedom from judgment should accelerate you to follow God away from your past and into a bright future.

FREE FROM JUDGEMENT

9 Are any of your choices making people around you question your Christianity? Are you controlled by any of your freedoms? Write a prayer asking God for forgiveness or protection from failing in your freedom.

_____

_____

_____

10 Are you using your freedom to practice evil, to do something God does not want his followers to do?

_____

_____

AT THE END OF THE WEEK ANSWER THESE QUESTIONS

What was the most meaningful statement(s) or scripture this week?	Reword the statement or scripture into a prayer of response to God.	What actions do you need to take in response to this week's study?
_____	_____	_____
_____	_____	_____
_____	_____	_____
_____	_____	_____
_____	_____	_____
_____	_____	_____

TRUTH 16

MEMORY VERSE

Don't let your hearts be troubled. Trust in God, and trust also in me. There is more than enough room in my Father's home. If this were not so, would I have told you that I am going to prepare a place for you? 3When everything is ready, I will come and get you, so that you will always be with me where I am.

John 14:1-3

Jesus Comes Back

He's Coming. Look forward. Be ready.

Jesus came to earth for the first time as a baby. He was born, and he grew up in a body like ours. He faced temptation and trial and lived among the world. His virgin birth was a miracle. As a young boy, he began to share the way for people to be reconciled to God. But, other than a few stories, we do not know much about Jesus' life until he was about thirty years old. Then, he called his first disciples and began to spread the message of salvation to all of Israel.

For three years, Jesus traveled, preached, healed, and shared the love and Good News of salvation. He died as a sacrifice providing forgiveness for all sin. Three days later, Jesus rose from that grave, conquering death once and for all. He walked the earth, taught, and encouraged people for forty days. Then, Jesus miraculously ascended to heaven in front of everyone!

Before his death, he prepared those that knew him, telling them he would come back and take all believers to heaven. Believers that were alive will miraculously ascend just as he did. Believers that had died will rise from the grave just as he did. Every believer will receive a new, holy sin-free body.

The description of his return runs throughout the Bible as Jesus, his disciples, and the prophets paint a vivid picture of the end times. His return will be majestic, frightening, miraculous, and amazing, all at the same time. God will judge everyone's faith and works. The corruption of the earth will end. Everything will be made righteous. God will restore the earth to the beauty and splendor of its beginning. And when the work of his return is complete, all who believe in Jesus will live forever in heaven.

The believers who walked with Jesus talked a lot about his return. Jesus did too. He wanted them to know the plan before he left earth. You and I need to know that plan as well. We need to be ready!

QUICK, SMART START

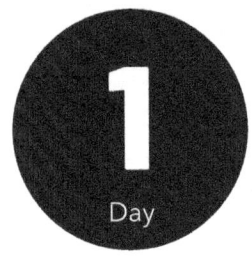

THE END TIMES

The disciples were astounded when Jesus ascended into heaven. He had told them he would die and did. He told them he would rise from the grave (called resurrection, see Luke 24:1-12) and did. Not only did Jesus come back to life, but he also spent the next forty days walking around, being seen, and teaching. Then while the disciples were still struggling to process his resurrection (see Luke 24:13-49), he rose into the sky (see Luke 24:50-53)! Can you imagine how overwhelming it must have been? Luke recorded Jesus' ascension in the Book of Acts.

Jesus has been taken from you into heaven, but someday he will return from heaven in the same way you saw him go!

> He was taken up into a cloud while they were watching, and they could no longer see him. As they strained to see him rising into heaven, two white-robed men suddenly stood among them. "Men of Galilee," they said, "why are you standing here staring into heaven? Jesus has been taken from you into heaven, but someday he will return from heaven in the same way you saw him go!"
>
> Acts 1:9-11

God sent two angels to reassure them of Jesus' words — Jesus would come back for them. And he would come back in the same way he left, in the clouds. The New Testament reveals much about Jesus' return, but the news was not all that new. People have known about Jesus' return since the beginning.

> It was also about these that Enoch, the seventh from Adam, prophesied, saying, "Behold, the Lord comes with ten thousands of his holy ones,
>
> Jude 1:14 ESV

Adam had a son named Seth, Seth had a son named Enosh, who had Kenan, who had Mahahalel, who had Jared, who had a son named Enoch. Enoch was so godly that God miraculously took him to heaven without dying (see Hebrews 11:5-6). Enoch, the sixth son from the beginning of man, knew about Jesus' return. He knew that Jesus would return with his holy ones to finish the earth's redemption. Thousands of years later, John wrote this same prophecy after being given a vision of the end times (see Revelation 19:11-15). The Old Testament prophet, Zechariah, also knew about Jesus' return (see Zechariah 14:3-5). The list goes on and on throughout the Old Testament. But perhaps the most straightforward understanding of what the return of Jesus will be like came from Jesus himself.

> Jesus told them, "Don't let anyone mislead you, for many will come in my name, claiming, 'I am the Messiah.' They will deceive many. And you will hear of wars and threats of wars, but don't panic. Yes, these things must take place, but the end won't follow immediately. Nation will go to war against nation, and kingdom against kingdom. There will be famines and earthquakes in many parts of the world. But all this is only the first of the birth pains, with more to come.
>
> "Then you will be arrested, persecuted, and killed. You will be hated all over the world because you are my followers. And many will turn away from me and betray and hate each other. And many false prophets will appear and will deceive many people. Sin will be rampant everywhere, and the love of many will grow cold. But the one who endures to the end will be saved. And the Good News about the Kingdom will be preached throughout the whole world, so that all nations will hear it; and then the end will come."
>
> Matthew 24:4-14

Zechariah 14:3,5

On that day his feet will stand on the Mount of Olives, east of Jerusalem...Then the Lord my God will come, and all his holy ones with him.

God showed John, a disciple of Jesus, what the end times would look like in an incredible vision. John's words echoed Jesus' words describing seven tough years before Jesus' return. John called it the tribulation. For seven years, God will unleash plagues, famine, and trials showing his glory and power to everyone. The tribulation will be intense. Jesus described it, saying,

> For there will be greater anguish than at any time since the world began. And it will never be so great again. In fact, unless that time of calamity is shortened, not a single person will survive. But it will be shortened for the sake of God's chosen ones.
>
> Matthew 24:21-22

But at the end of the trials, Jesus promised he would return.

QUICK, SMART START

> Immediately after the anguish of those days, the sun will be darkened, the moon will give no light, the stars will fall from the sky, and the powers in the heavens will be shaken.
>
> And then at last, the sign that the Son of Man is coming will appear in the heavens, and there will be deep mourning among all the peoples of the earth. And they will see the Son of Man coming on the clouds of heaven with power and great glory. And he will send out his angels with the mighty blast of a trumpet, and they will gather his chosen ones from all over the world—from the farthest ends of the earth and heaven.
>
> Matthew 24:29-31

Hebrews 10:12

But our High Priest offered himself to God as a single sacrifice for sins, good for all time.

Jesus' return will begin something new for all of us as God redeems the earth and all who believe in him. John recorded these words of Jesus about his return.

> And the one sitting on the throne said, "**Look, I am making everything new!**" And then he said to me, "Write this down, for what I tell you is trustworthy and true." And he also said, "It is finished! I am the Alpha and the Omega—the Beginning and the End. To all who are thirsty I will give freely from the springs of the water of life. All who are victorious will inherit all these blessings, and I will be their God, and they will be my children.
>
> Revelation 21:5-7

The book of Revelation (John's vision) is almost too much to process. God's description of heaven, worship, and our relationship with him is beyond comprehension. I imagine we will be as amazed as the disciples were when Jesus ascended into heaven. But Jesus' promise, God's promise, is that he will return and rule over the whole redeemed earth.

> Jesus said to them, "Truly, I say to you, in the new world, when the Son of Man will sit on his glorious throne, you who have followed me will also sit on twelve thrones, judging the twelve tribes of Israel. And everyone who has left houses or brothers or sisters or father or mother or children or lands, for my name's sake, will receive a hundredfold and will inherit eternal life. But many who are first will be last, and the last first.
>
> Matthew 19:28-30 ESV

So what will Jesus' return look like? There will be unbelievable trials, wars, and hatred before Jesus returns. Deception will abound as many claim to be the Messiah. Believers will be tempted by Satan to walk away from God. But, when Jesus returns, it will be glorious as he establishes a new home for all believers.

1 Write and memorize this week's memory verse.

_____

_____

_____

_____

Jesus' promise, God's promise, is that he will return and rule over the whole redeemed earth.

WHY IS JESUS RETURNING?

Jesus' return will complete God's plan to restore order, peace, and purity to the world. His power, majesty, justice, holiness, and love will be visible through every trial, tribulation, warning, and message of hope. The end times will be God's final, bold announcement to the world that he is the true God.

The first time Jesus came, he came to defeat the power of sin and death by offering himself as an eternal sacrifice (see Hebrews 10:1-12) for the penalty of sin (see Romans 6:23). But His second coming is for an entirely different purpose.

> So Christ, having been offered once to bear the sins of many, will appear a second time, not to deal with sin but to save those who are eagerly waiting for him.
>
> Hebrews 9:28 ESV

Romans 6:23

For the wages of sin is death, but the free gift of God is eternal life through Christ Jesus our Lord.

Jesus' return will begin a time where we will live in the direct presence of God. Jesus described it this way,

> And then they will see the Son of Man coming in clouds with great power and glory. And then he will send out the angels and gather his elect from the four winds, from the ends of the earth to the ends of heaven.
>
> Mark 13:26-27 ESV

> Don't let your hearts be troubled. Trust in God, and trust also in me. There is more than enough room in my Father's home. If this were not so, would I have told you that I am going to prepare a place for you? When everything is ready, I will come and get you, so that you will always be with me where I am.
>
> John 14:1-3

When the time is ready, Jesus will come back to save those who are waiting for him. If you ask, "Aren't Christians already saved?" you ask a great question. Christians are saved from the penalty of sin. Christians are saved and have been united with God's Holy Spirit. Christians have been made holy. But we still live in this corrupted world in a corrupted body. When Jesus returns, we will get a new, incorruptible body that matches your restored heart. We will no longer face temptations from our old selves. Peter described the completion of our salvation in his letter to new Christians.

> All praise to God, the Father of our Lord Jesus Christ. It is by his great mercy that we have been born again, because God raised Jesus Christ from the dead. Now we live with great expectation, and we have a priceless inheritance—an inheritance that is kept in heaven for you, pure and undefiled, beyond the reach of change and decay. And through your faith, God is protecting you by his power until you receive this salvation, which is ready to be revealed on the last day for all to see.
>
> 1 Peter 1:3-5

Paul explained it perfectly. Our earthly bodies are corrupted and can not inherit heaven. Jesus' fix is to transform our earthly bodies into heavenly bodies.

> Earthly people are like the earthly man, and heavenly people are like the heavenly man. Just as we are now like the earthly man, we will someday be like the heavenly man. What I am saying, dear brothers and sisters, is that our physical bodies cannot inherit the Kingdom of God. These dying bodies cannot inherit what will last forever.
>
> But let me reveal to you a wonderful secret. We will not all die, but we will all be transformed! It will happen in a moment, in the blink of an eye, when the last trumpet is blown. For when the trumpet sounds, those who have died will be raised to live forever. And we who are living will also be transformed. For our

dying bodies must be transformed into bodies that will never die; our mortal bodies must be transformed into immortal bodies.

1 Corinthians 15:48-53

Paul explains that believers who died before Jesus' return will be resurrected like Jesus. They will come out of their graves. The believers who are alive will be transformed instantly. Both dead and the living believers will get new, immortal, incorruptible bodies. John makes the same point. We are saved, but we are not yet like him in body.

> Beloved, we are God's children now, and what we will be has not yet appeared; but we know that when he appears we shall be like him, because we shall see him as he is.
>
> 1 John 3:2 ESV

Colossians 3:4

And when Christ, who is your life, is revealed to the whole world, you will share in all his glory.

The return of Jesus allows us to be with God, face to face, person to person, in his glory. (see **Colossians 3:4**) It is the completion of his plan to restore his creation to its original design.

 Read John's words about the second coming of Jesus below. Write what John saw in the blanks next to the verse numbers.

> Then I saw a new heaven and a new earth, for the old heaven and the old earth had disappeared. And the sea was also gone. ²And I saw the holy city, the new Jerusalem, coming down from God out of heaven like a bride beautifully dressed for her husband. ³I heard a loud shout from the throne, saying, "Look, God's home is now among his people! He will live with them, and they will be his people. God himself will be with them. ⁴He will wipe every tear from their eyes, and there will be no more death or sorrow or crying or pain. All these things are gone forever."
>
> Revelation 21:1-4

verse 1 _____

_____

verse 2 _____

_____

John 14:3

When everything is ready, I will come and get you, so that you will always be with me where I am.

verse 3 _____

_____

verse 4 _____

_____

God will create a new heaven and new earth (verse 1). There will be a new city where believers live and where God will be worshipped (verse 2). As in the Garden of Eden, before sin, God will live among his people (verse 3). There will be no more death, sorrow, crying, or pain (verse 4). Can you imagine standing in the presence of God? Can you imagine living forever without tears, trials, or temptations? It is going to be incredible! But, have you ever wondered why Jesus did not just take the believers with him? Why is Jesus waiting? What is he getting ready (see John 14:3)? Peter explained it in his final letter to Christians.

❸ Read Peter's words below, circling every word or phrase that has to do with time.

But you must not forget this one thing, dear friends: A day is like a thousand years to the Lord, and a thousand years is like a day. [9]The Lord isn't really being slow about his promise, as some people think. No, he is being patient for your sake. He does not want anyone to be destroyed, but wants everyone to repent. [10]But the day of the Lord will come as unexpectedly as a thief. Then the heavens will pass away with a terrible noise, and the very elements themselves will disappear in fire, and the earth and everything on it will be found to deserve judgment. [11]Since everything around us is going to be destroyed like this, what holy and godly lives you should live, [12]looking forward to the day of God and hurrying it along. On that day, he will set the heavens on fire, and the elements will melt away in the flames. [13]But we are looking forward to the new heavens and new earth he has promised, a world filled with God's righteousness. [14]And so, dear friends, while you are waiting for these things to happen, make every effort to be found living peaceful lives that are pure and blameless in his sight. [15]And remember, our Lord's patience gives people time to be saved.

2 Peter 3:8-15

4 Why is God waiting to send Jesus back to earth?

_____

_____

_____

When God creates the new world, the old world and all those who do not believe will be destroyed (verse 12). There will be a final judgment by God (verse 10). He will judge everyone regarding their faith and their works. No one will have an opportunity to believe after Jesus' return. Jesus is waiting, and we remain here so that those who do not know God can have a chance to be saved (verse 9, 15).

HOW WILL I BE JUDGED IN THE FINAL JUDGMENT?

Day 3

God will judge everyone (see 2 Corinthians 5:10, Romans 14:10-12) in the end. Still, your judgment will be different from those who do not believe. The final judgment asks, "Is this person a follower of Christ?" and gives unbelievers precisely what they want — separation from God. Jesus explained it this way,

> If anyone is ashamed of me and my message in these adulterous and sinful days, the Son of Man will be ashamed of that person when he returns in the glory of his Father with the holy angels.
> Mark 8:38

A believer's judgment will be different. Jesus said,

> Look, I am coming soon, bringing my reward with me to repay all people according to their deeds.
> Revelation 22:12

2 Corinthians 5:10

For we must all stand before Christ to be judged. We will each receive whatever we deserve for the good or evil we have done in this earthly body.

God will judge the works of each believer so that he can reward their good works. Paul explained it to the Corinthian church,

> No one can lay any other foundation than what has been laid—that is, Jesus Christ. If anyone builds on the foundation with gold, silver, costly stones, wood, hay, or straw, each one's work will become obvious, for the day will disclose it, because it will be revealed by fire; the fire will test the quality of each one's work. If anyone's work that he has built survives, he will receive a reward. If anyone's work is burned up, it will be lost, but he will be saved; yet it will be like an escape through fire.
>
> 1 Corinthians 3:11-15 HCSB

Your judgment will be an awards ceremony. Hopefully, you will not sit in the back, watching everyone else win all the rewards! What awards will be given? No one knows all the rewards God will hand out, but we know a few. Here's a quick list:

- Crown of Righteousness

> As for me, my life has already been poured out as an offering to God. The time of my death is near. I have fought the good fight, I have finished the race, and I have remained faithful. And now the prize awaits me—the crown of righteousness, which the Lord, the righteous Judge, will give me on the day of his return. And the prize is not just for me but for all who eagerly look forward to his appearing.
>
> 2 Timothy 4:6-8

- Crown of Life or Martyr's Crown

> God blesses those who patiently endure testing and temptation. Afterward they will receive the crown of life that God has promised to those who love him.
>
> James 1:12

> I know about your suffering and your poverty—but you are rich! I know the blasphemy of those opposing you. They say they are Jews, but they are not, because their synagogue belongs to Satan. Don't be afraid of what you are about to suffer. The devil will throw some of you into prison to test you. You will suffer for ten days. But if you remain faithful even when facing death, I will give you the crown of life.
>
> Revelation 2:9-10

- Rewards for Enduring Trial

> What blessings await you when people hate you and exclude you and mock you and curse you as evil because you follow the Son of Man. When that happens, be happy! Yes, leap for joy! For a great reward awaits you in heaven. And remember, their ancestors treated the ancient prophets that same way.
>
> Luke 6:22-23

- Crown of Glory – The Shepherd's Crown

> And now, a word to you who are elders in the churches. I, too, am an elder and a witness to the sufferings of Christ. And I, too, will share in his glory when he is revealed to the whole world. As a fellow elder, I appeal to you: Care for the flock that God has entrusted to you. Watch over it willingly, not grudgingly—not for what you will get out of it, but because you are eager to serve God. Don't lord it over the people assigned to your care, but lead them by your own good example. And when the Great Shepherd appears, you will receive a crown of never-ending glory and honor.
>
> 1 Peter 5:1-4

❺ Do you think it is ungodly to live with the idea of being rewarded for your good works?

_____

What does God's word teach?

_____

_____

_____

QUICK, SMART START

DO I HAVE TO LIVE THROUGH THE TRIBULATION?

God describes seven years of peace and seven years of trial during the end times. The trial period is called the tribulation. If you are dead before the tribulation, you will not have to live through it. But what if you are alive when the end times begin? Can you imagine living through all those trials, plagues, and judgments?

Some scholars believe that Christians who are alive when the end comes will be transformed and ascend to heaven before the tribulation. Other scholars are convinced that Christians will live through the tribulation and then ascend to heaven. Who is right?

Prophecy of the future can be troubling. There are times when prophecy is clear. There are times when prophecy is a bit more creative and symbolic. For example, Jewish leaders knew Jesus was coming the first time. They studied the prophecies of his coming and were convinced that Jesus would be an earthly king. They thought in earthly terms. They believed the prophecies pointed to him ruling the earth and subduing their enemies. They rejected him when Jesus told them that he was the King of Heaven, a spiritual king. The Jewish leaders could not adjust their belief of what would happen to what God was doing right in front of them. And many of them missed out on salvation.

Jesus' words and the prophecies of Jesus' return are complex. People argue over the rapture (being transformed and going directly to heaven without dying), the tribulation, and the timeline of the end times. Honest scholars know that no one knows exactly when believers will be raptured. But God's word is clear, believers will miraculously disappear and go to heaven.

> Two men will be working together in the field; one will be taken, the other left. Two women will be grinding flour at the mill; one will be taken, the other left.
> Matthew 24:40-41

> For the Lord himself will descend from heaven with a cry of command, with the voice of an archangel, and with the sound of the trumpet of God. And the dead in Christ will rise first. Then we who are alive, who are left, will be caught up together with

them in the clouds to meet the Lord in the air, and so we will always be with the Lord.

1 Thessalonians 4:16-17

I heard the best answer when I asked an old, wise mentor what he believed. He said, "I am going to prepare like I have to live through the tribulation and hope to God I don't have to!"

6 Are you living a life that prepares you for your arrival in heaven?

_____

7 How do you think you could prepare to live through the tribulation?

_____

_____

WHEN IS JESUS RETURNING?

Day 5

Like the rapture, no one knows when Jesus will return. While Jesus was on earth, he said it best,

> But concerning that day and hour no one knows, not even the angels of heaven, nor the Son, but the Father only.
> Matthew 24:36 ESV

What we do know is that the second coming will be unexpected. Even when the signs of Jesus' second coming begin, people will miss them and find themselves surprised. Jesus compared it to the people's surprise in the days of the Great Flood.

"When the Son of Man returns, it will be like it was in Noah's day. In those days before the flood, the people were enjoying banquets and parties and weddings right up to the time Noah entered his boat. People didn't realize what was going to happen until the flood came and swept them all away. That is the way it will be when the Son of Man comes."

Matthew 24:37-39

8 Why do you think people miss what God is doing around them?

_____

_____

For more than one hundred years, Noah built the Ark. He preached to people the entire time, but no one believed him. They thought he was crazy. And then the rain came. None of them were ready. Only eight believers got on the boat. People most often miss God because they are not looking for him. Even believers get so busy with their lives that they are blind to what their Father is doing around them. Other times, believers are like the Jewish people in Jesus' time. They reject what God is doing because it does not align with how they thought he would do it.

Immediately before the ascension, the disciples asked, "When are you coming back?" He answered,

> The Father alone has the authority to set those dates and times, and they are not for you to know. But you will receive power when the Holy Spirit comes upon you. And you will be my witnesses, telling people about me everywhere—in Jerusalem, throughout Judea, in Samaria, and to the ends of the earth.

Acts 1:7-8

Day 6: HOW DO I PREPARE FOR HIS RETURN?

Jesus' instruction was that we live in the power of the Spirit until we die or until he comes back. He wants us to live well on this earth and to make sure that everyone has the opportunity to hear about Him (see **Matthew 28:19-20**). Your most important work while you wait for Jesus is to be a witness of his love. You need to share the life you have been given with others. In Jesus' words,

You are the light of the world—like a city on a hilltop that cannot be hidden. No one lights a lamp and then puts it under a basket. Instead, a lamp is placed on a stand, where it gives light to everyone in the house. In the same way, let your good deeds shine out for all to see, so that everyone will praise your heavenly Father.

Matthew 5:14-16

You need to be the light. You need to take on the high calling of Jesus and be Jesus every minute, every hour, every day. You need to share the message. If people do not hear the message, they can never respond.

Everyone who calls on the name of the Lord will be saved. But how can they call on him to save them unless they believe in him? And how can they believe in him if they have never heard about him? And how can they hear about him unless someone tells them? And how will anyone go and tell them without being sent? That is why the Scriptures say, "How beautiful are the feet of messengers who bring good news!"

Romans 10:13-15

Matthew 28:19-20

go and make disciples of all the nations, baptizing them in the name of the Father and the Son and the Holy Spirit. Teach these new disciples to obey all the commands I have given you. And be sure of this: I am with you always, even to the end of the age.

9 List the people you are telling God's message of salvation. List the next three people you tell the Good News.

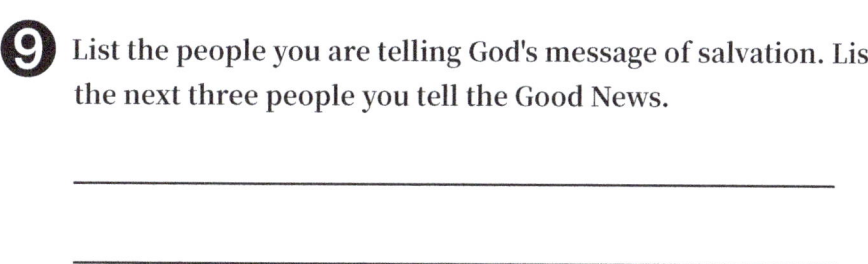

We are called to be messengers while we live on this earth. We are part of God's redemption plan. But while we wait, we also need to be very aware of the challenges of this world and the coming chaos. Jesus warned,

But watch yourselves lest your hearts be weighed down with dissipation and drunkenness and cares of this life, and that day will come upon you suddenly like a trap. For it will come upon all who dwell on the face of the whole earth. But stay awake at all times, praying that you may have strength to escape all these things that are going to take place, and to stand before the Son of Man.

Luke 21:34-36 ESV

James urged us to be hopeful and expectant and look toward the completion of our salvation like a farmer waits for crops to come in.

Win the world and win God's rewards.
- Phil Brown

> Therefore, brothers, be patient until the Lord's coming. See how the farmer waits for the precious fruit of the earth and is patient with it until it receives the early and the late rains. You also must be patient. Strengthen your hearts, because the Lord's coming is near.
>
> James 5:7-8 HCSB

John encouraged us to look toward the future and live pure lives while we wait on earth.

> Beloved, we are God's children now, and what we will be has not yet appeared; but we know that when he appears we shall be like him, because we shall see him as he is. And everyone who thus hopes in him purifies himself as he is pure.
>
> 1 John 3:2-3 ESV

> And now, little children, abide in him, so that when he appears we may have confidence and not shrink from him in shame at his coming.
>
> 1 John 2:28 ESV

Paul urged us to keep our eye on the ball as he reminded us that our loyalty, hope, and citizenship are in heaven with God.

> ...we are citizens of heaven, where the Lord Jesus Christ lives. And we are eagerly waiting for him to return as our Savior. He will take our weak mortal bodies and change them into glorious bodies like his own, using the same power with which he will bring everything under his control.
>
> Philippians 3:20-21

Hear Jesus' words as you read this last verse out loud.

> I am coming soon. Hold fast what you have, so that no one may seize your crown.
>
> Revelation 3:11 ESV

We need to do the work and be Jesus on earth while we are here. We need to share his message and call people to a better life of reconciliation and peace with God. We need to live well for others and for ourselves. Jesus wants us to be prepared, confident, and skilled to live abundant, rewarding lives here and now. My long-time friend and older mentor, Phil Brown, would say win the world and win God's rewards. And Phil knows what he is talking about.

❿ Are you looking to see God working around you, or are you merely waiting to get to heaven?

_____

_____

AT THE END OF THE WEEK ANSWER THESE QUESTIONS

What was the most meaningful statement(s) or scripture this week?	Reword the statement or scripture into a prayer of response to God.	What actions do you need to take in response to this week's study?

ABOUT US

Making the Disciple the Hero
of Their Story

Sustainable Discipleship is a team, a model, and a movement.

We are discipleship nerds. We are passionate about success in disciple making—for us, but more importantly, for the disciples. We study discipleship. We have studied discipleship in the Bible. We rediscovered how God made and makes disciples. We study the work of others—their successes and failures. We study the results of our discipleship. We measure, we test, and we experiment with new discipleship ideas and techniques.

Our team's single focus is helping others achieve success in making self-sustaining, self-replicating disciples. In other words, we are focused on helping others do well the one thing that God told us to do: make disciples.

Our approach is different than most. Our team does not produce discipleship courses or promote a specific program. We help disciple makers become rock stars, making self-sustaining, self-replicating followers of God in their context: large, small, contemporary, or traditional. We do this by combining God's method with a clear understanding of how people learn, think, and make decisions.

In other words, we make disciple makers and give them a simple, repeatable method to make more disciples than ever.

Sustainable Discipleship is also a movement of people passionate about helping Christians discover and live the abundant life that God promised. It is a movement to help people be prepared, confident, and skilled at following God. Churches of all denominations and characteristics are discovering passion, simplicity, and success in making disciples. Pastors and leaders are reaping the rewards. Disciples are succeeding.

If you want to talk discipleship, supercharge your discipleship, or join the movement, we are here. Sustainable Discipleship works. We guarantee it. And we have the data to back it up.

Doug
doug@sustainable-discipleship.com

ACKNOWLEDGEMENTS

None of us move forward, none of us learn without learning from those who go before and beside us. Quick Smart Start would never have come to be without a tribe of people from the past and present.

Thanks go out to the disciple-making superheroes at Three Taverns Church. They are my community, my church. They pray for me, support my writing, and champion the work of Sustainable Discipleship. They are my friends. They are the guinea pig subjects that test our new disciple-making ideas. They are wonderful and reflect what the church is meant to be.

Thanks to the entire Sustainable Discipleship team, who dreams big, picks me up when I wear out and pushes me to keep writing. Specifically, thanks to Bobbie Jo, Keith, Katie, and Jaime, who reviewed, challenged, and edited this book. Thanks to Tim, who keeps things running at church so we can invest in a disciple-making movement. And, if I may thank someone twice, I need to thank Jaime, our entrepreneurial leader handling the details behind the scenes.

Thanks to Bob Canuette, my champion and hero in the faith, who helped me when I was young. I miss Bob. Thanks to Milan Beasley, who invested in me at the start. Thanks to Nathanael, who edited the first two drafts of this work over the years. And, thanks to Phil Brown, my never-alone friend.

Phil is the pastor emeritus of Monterrey Baptist Church and leader emeritus of RIBBI Mexico, a network of churches making disciples. He continues to teach and write curricula to advance the kingdom. He is unstoppable. Phil was making disciples long before I got out of my disciple-making diaper. I credit and quote him in every discipleship book. I talk about him to those who dream of making disciples. Phil helped me put words on the first seven steps we found in discipleship. He challenged my research, exposing it to his years of practice. The sixteen truths he taught his disciples lined up with the questions ours were asking. Again, Phil was ahead of us. His booklet became the foundation of Quick Smart Start.

Quick Smart Start would never have happened without all these friends.

ABOUT THE AUTHOR

Doug Burrier is the founder of Different.ly, a decision science consulting firm that helps leaders, churches, and corporations make better decisions. Doug has a degree is decision sciences, a PhD in Christian leadership, and a master in biblical studies. He has researched, designed, and carried out discipleship for over twenty years as the pastor of Three Taverns Church, where he created the highly successful sustainable-discipleship model. Doug writes about discipleship from his home in Acworth, Georgia, where he lives with his wife and two dogs.

Doug is passionate about discipleship and regularly helps churches define and design successful disciple-making processes as a part of the Sustainable Discipleship's online learning, coaching, and private workshops. Doug is a high-energy, creative speaker. He thrives at unlocking the secrets of how to make and be disciples. To learn more or book Doug for your team or next event, email team@sustainable-discipleship.com.

MORE RESOURCES

How to Make Disciples: A Simple, Proven Model for Making Self-Sustaining Followers of God
— Printed, ebook, and audio available on Amazon, Apple, Audible and at sustainable-discipleship.com/the-book.

Well Made, Well Done: How to Know You've Succeeded in Making Disciples
— Printed, ebook, and audio available on Amazon, Apple, Audible.

Ultra Discipleship: Fourteen Predictable Checkpoints in Disciple Making
— Available Winter 2023

Be(e) Discipleship: Disciple-Making as a Solution to Colony Collapse in the Church
— Available Fall 2023

The Discipleship Pathway: Discovering the Highly Predictable Steps on the Way to Spiritual Maturity
— Available at sustainable-discipleship.com

Live Workshops: Be a Disciple-Making Superhero
— Get started or hone your craft and become a disciple-making superhero with a public, private or hosted workshop. Learn more at sustainable-discipleship.com.

Inspiration and Design Coaching
— Let us inspire your team, evaluate your process, or help you launch a sustainable-discipleship plan. Email us at team@sustainable-discipleship.com.

Made in the USA
Monee, IL
01 February 2024

52044933R00142